KNEELING IN SPIRIT

KNEELING IN SPIRIT
Disabled Submissives

Edited by Raven Kaldera

Alfred Press
Hubbardston, Massachusetts

Alfred Press
12 Simond Hill Road
Hubbardston, MA 01452

Kneeling In Spirit: Disabled Submissives
© 2013 Edited by Raven Kaldera
ISBN 978-0-9828794-5-0

Cover Photography by John Riedell

Printed in cooperation with
Lulu Enterprises, Inc.
860 Aviation Parkway, Suite 300
Morrisville, NC 27560

Dedicated to V-boy,
guinea pig boy,
beta tester of my theories,
who proved that it would really work out.

Contents

Foreword

When people think of the archetypal slave, most of them think of someone with a beautiful—and perhaps close to perfect—body, who could be shown off on the mythical slave auction block and everyone would bid a high price. They don't usually picture someone with crutches, or a wheelchair, or who is lacking various senses—that is, unless that's specifically their kink. They certainly don't picture someone with a chronic illness who will have days where they can't get out of bed due to pain. If they do connect the concepts of a defective body and consensual slavery or service, they tend to imagine the s-type as worthless, the lowest of the low, certainly not "valuable property". And yet disabilities happen. Any of us could be run over by a bus and end up in bad shape, and we would not be worthless. After all, what's valuable property is in the eye of the dominant beholder, and we dominants are a notoriously variable lot.

This book came about as a natural companion to the first book in this series—*Hell On Wheels: Disabled Dominants*. I knew that I had to follow it up with something for the people on the other side, although I didn't know exactly how to navigate the issue. I'd been a disabled dominant for some time, with a wonderful (and able-bodied) slaveboy who saw to my needs. I didn't honestly have a lot of experience with managing someone who had serious physical problems, and I worried a bit that I wouldn't actually be qualified to edit this anthology, even with all the wonderful people who sent in their writing for the world to see.

Then the Universe, of course, decided to drop a disabled submissive in my lap. My slaveboy and I had been looking for a second boy, someone to help out and fill in the cracks when the two of us were completely overworked. When a boy applied who generally fit our other criteria, we took him under consideration for service to me—and then discovered that he had severe fibromyalgia that had crippled him off and on since his early teens. We did a bit of worrying as to whether he'd be able to handle the job of being in service to me, but we decided cautiously to go ahead with the project. I knew a lot about managing a troublesome body; I had one.

Certainly I could help manage someone else's? After all, how hard could it be?

If you're hoping that those words were a lead-in to how it was far more of a struggle than I thought it would be, you'd be wrong. Actually, it went more smoothly than I hoped. There was some skepticism on the part of people who surrounded us—one individual, upon hearing of my new boy's problems, said, "Don't keep that one—hold out for someone who can do the heavy farm chores!" Still, I felt that if I was really the creative master that I said I was, I should be able to figure out how to find ways to make the relationship feel like it was worthwhile to both of us. So far, I think we've succeeded; you can read his side of the story—which is more important here—later in this book.

I will say, though, that the most important piece of training I undertook with him was his ability to accurately assess and communicate his physical state at any given time. This is a theme that plays out again throughout this book—part of transparency is total honesty about the ups and downs of the s-type's condition on any given day. That's not just a matter of control and privacy invasion (one of the tried-and-true "mindset" tools of the master); it's about making the best use of your human resource, which isn't possible if you don't know what you're dealing with from day to day. This is especially crucial when you're dealing with a fluctuating illness that could be all over the charts in a week's time. I think that masters of disabled submissives have to learn much more quickly to assess a situation and give an appropriate order, or it all falls apart very quickly. To make it work, though, the s-type needs to get good at it as well.

In the past, I've often said that the core of the master's job is risk assessment. When do you push them towards—or past—their stated limits, because you have a gut feeling that they could do more and go further than they believe themselves capable of? When do you back off and respect those limits, because they'll break if you don't? When do you set limits for them that are even more restricting than what they believe themselves capable of, because you feel that they overcommit and overestimate their abilities? In other words, when do you believe that they know best about their own capabilities? When do you decide that they don't necessarily have it right, and you are seeing something that they can't ... and you're in a position to enforce it?

That's what I mean about risk assessment, and it is even more crucial when you as the master are dealing with a disabled submissive or slave ... and even more frightening. When you actually do have the potential to break them in even worse ways than simple mental stress, it makes each of these decisions even larger and more dangerous. Some dominants may back off in the face of all this uncertainty, enough that the s-type feels even more incompetent and useless. As many of the essays in this book stress, if you can get regular honest reports on their condition, and you are willing to be creative and think outside the box, you can find ways that they can be of service and of pleasure that are more than just makework or humoring them.

The first step—which is, again, stressed in many of the essays here—is for the dominant to learn everything they can about their s-type's condition, and from sources of information other than simply their s-type. Talk to their doctors (with them present to give permission). Read up on it. Talk to other people with similar conditions. Become something of an expert on it. If they are yours, so are their problems. If you own them, you own that disability as well, and the first and best thing you can do is to stuff your head with as much preparatory information as you can.

On top of all the actual details of the s-type's disability, one must also take into account their past history with other people's attitudes toward that disability. If they've had it all their life, were they encouraged to do things in spite of their problems, or were they sheltered and discouraged from having challenging experiences? Were they saddled with a self-image of competence or fragility? Were their issues believed or scoffed at? Were they able to get help when they needed it, or did they have to make a fuss to get anyone to take them seriously? Conversely, if their disability came on later in life, what assumptions and self-images were they carrying which had to be demolished, or are perhaps lingering around to make them feel bad about themselves? Each of these points must be taken into account when a dominant takes on a disabled submissive or slave, and should shape their handling of that particular s-type.

As with the first anthology in this series, *Hell on Wheels: Disabled Dominants*, when I put out the call for submissions I got a lot of complaints from s-types who were not in relationships, and blamed that on their disabilities—"No one wants a slave who can't kneel, or carry, or who is in a wheelchair, or who needs to spend a lot of time in bed, or who can't put their body into certain positions for sex, or who can't handle much in the way of SM and play." No one, was the unspoken statement, wants a slave who is more submissive to the constraints of their condition than to any dominant.

One of the other complaints that I got frequently during these interviews was from submissives who had become disabled after entering a power dynamic with their significant other, and the partner decided that the power dynamic was no longer viable given their physical obstacles. "Twysted", who was abandoned by her dominant after being diagnosed with multiple sclerosis and a stroke disorder, talks about how her partner handled it and what could have been done differently:

> He was really unable to cope with the diagnosis. His solution was basically to give up D/s, because I was "broken". Needless to say, I was beyond myself trying to cope with the pain, both mental and physical, in addition to dealing with his issues over it all. But in the long run I've become a much stronger person than before. So I have complications? Well, life goes on and I'm not ready to lay down and play dead.
>
> What could he have done differently? He could have tried to understand that I was no different than the before the diagnosis; we just had a name for it now. Instead of just giving up on everything, he could have read, learned, and armed himself with knowledge so that he could have adapted to situations better as they arose.

Instead of him saying to me "You're broken now, and I can't fix you, so I need to put you on a pedestal like a china doll that's been mended," he could have learned that it simply meant I'd have bad days and good days (and sometimes perhaps bad weeks), but I was still capable of being a good sub, and even capable of S/M sometimes as well. If you have a favorite toy that is old and more fragile, you don't throw it away if you love it enough. You just learn to be more careful and gentle when you play with it.

I think that a good structure could have been easily achieved. Just ask how I am feeling and listen to the answer, then plan the day/evening/event from there. For me, I needed to learn to be clear about my current condition, understand that there were times I just couldn't do something, and it was up to me to say so, and not try to hide the pain or exhaustion and do it anyway. Perhaps he could have taken on the chore of cooking a couple of nights a week, or even just on the nights I couldn't do it. Instead, his solution was to just fend for himself, not worry about anyone else in the house, and say "You don't have too cook; everyone can get something themselves." (I had kids still at home at this time, and you can imagine what it was like when four kids and three adults were all doing their own thing in the kitchen at once.)

Perhaps he could have made sure that his laundry was out by the machine (we had a nice laundry room that I could even use sitting down, as everything was front loading), so that I wouldn't have had to carry it. (His solution was just to do his own laundry, still leaving me to carry my own, the kids', the towels, bed linens, etc., or leave it undone if I couldn't manage.) Little things go a long way, but even if those weren't acceptable solutions, surely we could have figured something out. It's important to let the person do what they can while they can still do something. If you take everything away from them, they may as well lay down and play dead.

I feel that I have a lot yet to give to the right Master, but I need a loving, understanding Dominant that isn't selfish about his needs/wants to the point of being unable to find a compromise. I need one that will work to understand and adapt to what I am dealing with, and find ways to make it all work... *together.*

I thought I lost everything when I was diagnosed. But ten years later, I know that I've gained so much from my experiences. I'm much better at life now, much more resilient. I wish he'd been resilient as well.

This was hardly a unique story, unfortunately. However, I also heard from slaves and submissives who were in perfectly good power exchange relationships, and had simply adapted their lifestyles to find ways in which both parties could still get at least some of their needs met. In some cases the master controlled the slave's health decisions; in others the submissive dealt with their own health care and the dominant simply expected them to do their best. In every one of these, there was a lot of communication about what could be expected of the s-type at any given time, and a lot of compassion flowing in both directions.

Recently I was on a panel about disability and Master/slave relationships at a major conference. My co-panelists included a dominant woman who used crutches and sometimes a wheelchair after a spinal injury, and a blind female slave. The audience seemed to be full of slaves and submissives who had come down with some injury or disability that prevented them from doing much of the physical labor of serving, and many of them wept as they described their crisis of self-esteem. None of them said that their masters were throwing them out; the problem seemed to be entirely in their own hearts. They had built their image of themselves as good submissives or slaves on their ability to provide specific services for their masters and mistresses, and when they were unable to achieve those goals, the bottom fell out of their self-image. They felt worthless, and were sure that sooner or later their dominants would realize their worthlessness as well.

It occurred to me, while they were speaking, how much value the people in some areas of the M/s demographic place on service, and specifically active service of the task-oriented variety. As a disabled master, service is crucially important to me—it's what makes my life livable, actually. However, I've always felt that there were two equally important values in D/s and M/s, and only one of them is service. The other one is control, and being controlled. Different masters and slaves prefer to be on different areas of the spectrum between service and control, and we've often said that having the right "fit" as to which you prefer is one of the key values that create compatibility in power dynamic relationships. However, while a physically disabled s-type may be limited in the amount of service they can provide, they can always provide obedience.

This was the point that my fellow dominant panelist and I attempted to make to the unhappy s-types in the audience. *Never underestimate the power of just plan obeying. Never underestimate how much we M-types like to hear "Yes, Sir," "Yes, Ma'am."* No matter how important being served may be to us, there's a reason why we decided that we wanted to be in charge. We get a deep sense of satisfaction just from saying, "You've done enough—I can see that you're hurting. Go lie down. Now!" ... and seeing it done, immediately, without argument. It's possible that we even like that better than seeing whatever it was that you couldn't do get done.

One note on terminology: Several of the authors in this anthology, myself included, will often use the word "spoons" to indicate a discrete unit of body energy. This analogy was first made by Christine Miserandino, the creator of the website http://www.butyoudontlooksick.com, an online support network for people with chronic illnesses. She describes the "spoon theory" in an article on the website, where she tells the story of being in a late-night diner and trying to explain to a friend what it was like to live with a chronic illness. She grabbed up the spoons from nearby tables and used them as an abstract example — each spoon represented a unit of energy needed to do some small and basic thing such as wash, dress, or eat — and some days there weren't enough "spoons" to do much of anything. Since then, many people with chronic illnesses and disabilities that impact their energy levels (and thus their ability to manage everyday activities) have referred to their "units of energy" as "spoons", as in "I've only got two spoons left, so I'd better get home while I can still drive." People now wish each other more spoons, and even give away little spoon-shaped pins as gifts. You'll see that term used throughout the book by various authors who struggle daily to make the most of their limited spoons.

As I wrote in the first book in this series, *Hell On Wheels*: May you all be as healthy as it's possible to be, with more spoons than you ever expected, and have joy in bed and out of it, in the dungeon and out of it, in the community and out of it, in the circle of family and out of it, and in each others' hearts and minds.

RAVEN KALDERA
JANUARY, 2013

Being A Disabled Submissive

The Use Of Trusting

V-Boy

Since my kindergarten years, the chronic pain of fibromyalgia has been my constant companion in some form or another. Even when it's not flaring, it's always been there, keeping me company through the coming and going of various other conditions that were rectified via minor surgeries, lifestyle changes, and medication. Occasionally it adds on new triggers and symptoms just as I was getting a grasp of the old ones, because fibromyalgia seems to get off on being mysterious. This became a huge factor in my inability to reliably predict my body's capabilities on a regular basis, and the very nature of having fluctuating pain that could not be medically proven has led to a great deal of doubt about my honesty, first from others and then eventually from my own fears. I found fibromyalgia to be a useless thing that did nothing but make my existence more difficult. As it affected every facet of my life in some defining way, it then shared that useless feeling with me. And as I have learned, if anything is going to haunt a service-oriented person, it's being Useless.

If the world Useless makes you cringe, then we have some solid common ground. It's not my favorite word, and nowhere near my favorite state of mind, so it might seem that my call to service could have easily backfired. Initially, I was drawn to submissive service from a spiritual perspective that has become stronger as time has gone on, and I most certainly didn't mind my new kinky lifestyle being the avenue for finding someone to serve. As a matter of fact, one previously-not-practical use of my fibromyalgia showed itself pretty early on: A high sensitivity paired with a high pain tolerance.

So it was with a slightly more secure feeling about the possibilities of working with my chronic pain in the non-vanilla world that I contacted someone who seemed to be looking for the service I wanted to offer, and now I'm writing this piece at his request. My general feeling of Use has managed to tip from Useless well into Useful as my service to him has continued, but there were years of untouched mental cleanup I had to do, and am still doing, to stay in this mindset on a regular basis.

The biggest personal roadblock I have to deal with is those times of feeling Useless that in turn cause me to be even more useless than whatever triggered the feeling in the first place. That's just an annoying cycle that can make anyone end up in a place that is no good, and even more so when one has a condition like fibromyalgia. Two of the most across-the-board triggers of fibromyalgia flares seem to be stress and depression, so this can result in a flare that feeds on the mental insecurity it causes in a self-perpetuating loop, which means one simply needs to break the cycle and it will help them feel at least a little better. But as with any self-feeding cycle, the question is, "Oh, come on, don't you think I'd be stopping it already if I could?" or, when not currently in the middle of such a situation, "How would I go about that?"

One important point I stumbled upon was how much it means to have my self-evaluations be trusted. Raven will regularly ask me for reports on what I feel up to at a particular time, and I am expected to take a moment to check in with my body and honestly answer; then I am given some things I can do that are within my stated limits. Towards the beginning, I kept feeling a little off-kilter after these exchanges and it took me some time to figure out why.

It was because of the trust in his answer. It was always a full acceptance of my stated ability, not "Are you sure you can't do just a little more?" or "You were able to do a similar action earlier, why not now?", which would make me doubt myself, then feel bad when I still couldn't follow through. Yet if I did actually overestimate my ability, I was again asked for a self-evaluation, then troubleshooting was done for the future. Sitting around feeling like a disappointment, while being extra encouragement to not *want* to repeat that particular failure, was not especially productive in actually fixing it or keeping it from happening again.

But this trust needed to go both ways. While he trusted that I was communicating my capabilities, I needed to also trust that he was satisfied with what I could manage to do. Around the time I was taken under consideration for service, my life started doing some... rearranging. The highlights were long-time-coming ruptures in relationships with lovers, my parents, and childhood friends, losing my small job at my church, becoming homeless, and facing down old emotional triggers I thought were well under control. Then on top of all this, I was watching my health act in strange new ways, particularly with weather-triggered flares, as well as coming down with a surprisingly bad case of thrush after a difficult tonsillectomy.

Needless to say, I was questioning pretty early on why anyone, let alone someone who was considering me for my service, would keep me around when things were such a mess. At the very least I knew that *I* was getting tired of all this! But I was being kept around, sometimes even tucked away upstairs until my health cleared up, which meant that these insecurities were not being caused by any outside influence. They were fully crafted of my own inner gunk. This is when I came up with the Concept of Investment.

The Concept of Investment is a wonderfully simple tool that manages to nip many of my worries in the bud. First, I clarify with myself what I'm actually feeling upset about. For instance, perhaps my body's limit for the day was far less than I thought, or I needed a task to be altered or put off to be able to do any work on it, or I needed to spend a full day curled up in bed. And why am I feeling upset? Because I'm feeling like I'm more trouble than I'm worth. I'm feeling years of shaming reminding me how I'm more a burden than any sort of help. I'm feeling Useless.

With my mindset acknowledged, the second step is establishing a simple fact: he has made an investment in me by considering me for, and then taking me into, his service. He has invested time, energy, resources, and trust so that I can better serve him. But here I am, not being able to serve as much as someone more able-bodied could. I'm a physical mess and after a lifetime of this, I'm quite aware that it's not magically changing anytime soon. (Well, at least not for the better.)

Then in the final step I ask myself, "Where did I get the idea that I decide what he wants?" Because honestly, that's what it boils down to. I may be insecure and think little of what I have to offer when I'm in those dark places, but he did take me into service, and it was most certainly not for my dependable health. So this is where I need to trust. I trust that he took me into service because he was getting some worthwhile return on his investment. Most importantly, I need to trust that he is continuing to do so, and that if there were a huge problem with it, he'd tell me.

Seriously, though, at no other time would I ever even consider turning to him and saying, "No, actually, you're obviously lying to me about what you want. You've got this service thing all wrong." Why would this be any different?

So sometimes during a small flare I need to take constant breaks from a task so that I don't completely burn out. Or I need to go eat something because my blood pressure dropped. Or I've been sent to do nothing but sleep until I'm no longer ill. If I'm going to offer myself in service, then I need to take care of the body doing the work. He trusts that I am doing my best, and I trust that what he has seen to be my best is enough of a return, no matter how Useless I'm feeling.

It's Possible

bijohninohio

I'm a forty-one-year-old bisexual male domestic submissive. That means that I generally take care of the cooking, the cleaning, the laundry, and anything else to do with running the home. In addition, I've had two strokes, leaving me weak on the right side and in constant pain. I've had surgery on my right knee, changing the length of my leg. I also have a bad back from a fall out of a chair—a cousin pulled the chair out from under me as a joke, not realizing how dangerous the act really would be for me. The fall caused my spine to twist instead of compressing, and the combination of the surgery and the fall have caused my back to strain in a different direction as I was growing. The twist has caused my hips to be angled as well, making it difficult and painful to sit for long periods of time without moving.

I've had multiple relationships with women, and dabbled with guys at one time. I met and married a wonderful girl, and we were together for about a year when our son was born. Shortly afterward, her family convinced her that I was not a good person for her, and we ended up separating and eventually divorcing. I didn't get into the BDSM world until after a major breakup with my next partner, the mother of my three youngest children. We were together for twelve years when she suddenly decided that she was no longer in love with me, moved out, and very quickly married another guy that she claimed she had been seeing for most of our relationship. It was during this relationship that I had my first stroke. Unfortunately, she did not adapt well to my becoming disabled, and we had many arguments about income. She had gotten disability for anxiety and depression, but didn't believe that I should get disability for my stroke. She also wanted me away from home for periods of time, and I later found out that this was for playing around with other men during my working times.

After another dry spell, I became friends with my ex-wife again, and one day we had a long conversation about BDSM. Since she knew me quite well, she let me into some secrets in her private life. I learned that she was a submissive and had a Master, and she referred me to the website where she and her Master were on. Upon reading and talking with multiple people, we decided that I was indeed a submissive and needed to find a Mistress. After a long search I found my current Madam, who took me on to train. My Madam has worked with me through my disabilities, through the good days and bad days, and continues to believe in me, something I have not had in my past.

I was already disabled before I met my Madam. I actually traveled twenty-six hundred miles across the United States to meet her, and we have been together ever since. As of 2012, it has been two years. We experimented in the beginning to test my limits, and as I continued to worsen, we limited our activities to those days when I felt good enough, and we kept our play short so as not to overwork my body. Even after two years, our play times continue to get more and more limited, as I have to deal with more and more pain. Madam continues to try and help me as much as she can. Our relationship contains aspects of both service and control—I do domestic service for my Madam, but she also has control over my sexual outlets, and my orgasms. I must ask permission to have an orgasm.

Almost everything in life becomes more and more difficult as days go by. Because of the pain and weakness in my hip and back, walking, standing, even sitting for periods of time become a problem. I still try to do dishes and laundry as my chores, but there are days when I can't stand at the sink long enough to do them. We try to do grocery runs on good days, and try to use those days as time to get away from the house for as long as I can stand. We avoid walking as much as possible, or try to find other options like renting a motorized scooter so that we could spend the day at the zoo. When I am having a physically bad day, I generally tend to stay in bed or do absolutely nothing after getting up. Madam has accepted the fact that I have these days, and she will usually do the chores herself that day, or else leave them until I am able to do them.

We handle my medical decisions together. Since my Madam is in a medical field, I value her input about my health. Sometimes she will make suggestions, but then it is ultimately my decision to follow through with it or not. However, if I don't follow through and my health does deteriorate, then she will take control and handle the situation herself.

I have not done any play outside our home, and I have not been to any community events. I don't believe that my disability would make a difference in whether I would take part or not, but the problem is that I do have a social fear of people, and I tend to stay away from crowded places. There's not really any help event organizers could give to make things easier for me, as I am able to go most places when I'm not hurting. If I'm hurting, I tend to just not go anyplace.

When a new would-be sub is looking for a Dominant, they need to be sure and be absolutely open about their disability. If the Dominant still decides to take on that sub, despite their disabilities, then that shows that it is a caring Dominant willing to work with that sub. Communication is very key to all aspects, especially during the beginning stages of a relationship. I would also recommend that the sub not be afraid to tell other people about their disabilities as well. They may be surprised at the support they will get from others.

If a would-be Dominant is talking to a disabled sub, they need to remember that even though they have a disability, they are still human, and more than likely can have their feelings hurt much easier than someone without disabilities. Disabled subs can end up more loyal, in my opinion, because we will try to overcome our disabilities to make the Dominant happy in any way we possibly can. If there's anything I want people to understand, it is to please always understand that even disabled people have desires to be a submissive or a Dominant. Be sure to give them their chance.

Meeting The Challenge

egg

I'm a 41-year-old female slave living in the Midwest. I have a Master's degree (no pun intended) and was a working professional in my field for fifteen years. In my younger days I studied martial arts and music, and I love to write. My politics are liberal, my spirituality is new age-based and I'm a nerdy girl.

The definition of the submissive versus a slave, for me, has to be up there with the chicken and the egg question. I consider myself a slave. I can't think of a thing I wouldn't do for my HusDom, but then again I wouldn't have accepted a collar from anyone I feared would ask something of me that I felt I couldn't give. I know this may not equate to the definitions and terms that others use, but I'm his slave, he's my Master. It works for us.

We just celebrated our fifth wedding anniversary and I've proudly worn his collar for the last six years. Master has me on a very long leash, which has allowed this to work for both of us. We're a 24/7 couple, but I don't live in sub-space. Our relationship looks like just about any other happy couple's relationship out in public. Every now and then if you look closely you might see a hair tug or slap on the ass, but we're basically just two crazy kids in love. At home behind closed doors we observe the rituals and protocol that have shaped our relationship.

I was in my mid-twenties when I first gained enough nerve to explore whether any of the kinky things in my head were actually things I wanted to do. I found a lot of information online, attended the Slosh, and was active in the AOL chat room that most of the people at the Slosh used to communicate on a nightly basis. I met people, dated, had some play dates and made some really good friends. I visited the local clubs and went to a handful of the convention-like events. There were a few serious relationships along the way until I met the man who would eventually collar and marry me. I knew after our first weekend together that he was the one I was going to marry, but I didn't mention that until very recently. That kind of talk scares people away, especially if it's after a second date.

My right knee became arthritic in 2010 to the point of ending my career, drastically lowering my income and ability to work. In the fall of 2011 I learned that my left knee was completely devoid of cartilage. On bad days I need to use a walker, occasionally use a cane and rely on a mobility scooter just to get out of the apartment. In addition, I have very luckily lived through two pulmonary embolisms, which also present their own set of challenges and limitations.

I considered myself a slave before my knees completely went out on me. When I first met my Master, I was still in good enough shape to attend martial arts classes, and now just walking across the apartment is a challenge at times. My self-image has definitely changed as a result. I am physically unable to do things I used to be able to do and there have been times when I've considered myself "less than" as a result of not being able-bodied enough to do those things. I think back to my very beginnings in the scene and wish I could somehow give my Master the body I had in my twenties that was able to do more things—kneel, bend, be tied up for long periods of time, stand for more than thirty seconds without discomfort and so on. However, the reality of the situation is that we are here and now in this time, and I do my best according to my abilities.

Emotionally this has been a strain on each of us in different ways. When the situation gets the better of me it can be frustrating, depressing and a no-win situation. I try not to let myself go to the pity parties. However, I don't see that same kind of frustration from Master. He's never groaned about what I can't do for him anymore and has been nothing but loving and supportive. In fact, he has been my champion as a result of these changes in my physical abilities. On the days when things are really, really bad for me, when even the hardcore prescription pain killers can't bring any relief, it probably looks more like he's the slave and I'm the Dominant. But people who assumed this would be wrong.

Adaptation is the challenge that we are now addressing, and mostly at this point its figuring out the literal mechanics. We do not play as often as we used to, and when we do, it's not for hours at a time as it had been in the past. Sex and play are difficult at best. The spirit is more than willing, but these knees aren't going to handle anything interesting. We're doing our best to figure out how to do all the things we want to do. Bondage is pretty much out the window with the blood clots/embolisms, and I have a tendency to bruise a lot easier than before because of the medication. Sometimes it hurts just to lie face down on the bed, so a lot of our past activities have been altered or eliminated altogether. Some activities have been placed on hold until we can come up with a reasonable accommodation.

There is no serving on a very bad day. There's graceful acceptance of Master's love and help if I'm having a very bad day. However, our relationship is about service as well as control; there are some things I can do, and I do them. Actually, I'd like to think it's a healthy mix of both. If I had to pick one, though, I'd say our relationship is more about control.

When you have trouble with mobility, everything is difficult. Everything needs to be considered before any action is taken. I have a walker and a cane on my side of the bed. They are there in case I need help just to get out of bed. We have a bath bench in the shower, as I can't stand in the tub and take a shower. There is a chair in the kitchen that aids in cooking, loading and emptying the dishwasher, putting away groceries and so on. Many of the items I need in the kitchen I've tried to place or arrange at a level that is accessible from a sitting position. There is a laundry basket on my side of the bed, as standing to put laundry in the other basket is taxing. Master does the laundry; I fold and he usually puts most of it away. I do my best to clean house via a rolling chair, but I don't have a prayer when it comes to the bathtub! When we can afford it, this is a chore I'd like to outsource.

Leaving the apartment is an entirely different set of concerns. The bank, a couple stores and the gym are close enough that I can reach those locations independently on my mobility scooter when it is functioning properly and the weather is cooperating. We don't have a lift for the scooter for our van, so I can only go so far without it. I often try to look online at an unfamiliar location to see if it is even going to be doable for me and have missed out on some activities as a result. Otherwise, I know the layout of the places I go, which stores have carts you can borrow, which restaurants have good seating close to the door, which movie theatre is comfortable and which merchants tolerate the disabled. I've been surprised by the intolerance more than anything. You'd think they were paying me for goods and services with the attitude I sometimes receive.

I could not remain in the same career I had before my knees went out, and we are now living on about a third of the money we used to have coming in every month. I've learned how to coupon out of necessity, and to stretch every penny as far as it will go. We moved from a two-floor walk up condominium in a classy suburb to a cheaper apartment building with an elevator. I've learned how to apply for disability, where the food pantries are, and how to ask for food stamps. I've found a new career, one that I can perform at home, but the pay is very low for the amount of work I actually do. I also learned how to live without health insurance for a short period of time, and am convinced more than ever that we absolutely need reform in the U.S. concerning the ability of every man, woman and child to receive medical attention regardless of monetary situation.

I've also developed a real sense of gratitude in all of this. I know it's a cliché, but it's really easy to appreciate what you don't have any more. I've learned to count the blessings I do have, to stop taking things for granted and reshape some of my thinking.

For someone who suddenly found themselves in the same situation as me, I would advise getting over any sense of shame/pride/fear that is not actually helping you, and to seek out every single source of support and help that you can find. There is a lot of help out there if you have the time and patience to look for it. Paperwork is a nightmare. Be prepared for government agencies to make you bend over backwards to get what you need. You may have more time than money. Learn to use your time like money. Get a copy of anything and everything that has any relation to your disability and keep those papers organized. Turn in your forms on time. Be open and honest with people you care about concerning your situation. Make sure your Dominant knows if there is a problem and what, if anything, they can do to help you. (I've been told Masters aren't mind-readers!)

If you're a disabled submissive and you want to be in a power exchange relationship, don't let your disability get you down! Get out, meet people, go to events, be yourself, don't do anything you don't want to do, learn everything you can about this lifestyle, keep a journal, make a list of your non-negotiables, know your limitations, have fun. I do know that getting out to BDSM events is rough. I know that there is one club in Chicago where I could not go because of all the stairs. It would kill me just to attempt to get up those stairs. The other clubs are accessible, as I remember, and the larger community events have been willing to make accommodations—i.e. allowing people to use an elevator to get to the play space. We don't have a very active public life, but now that I have a lot more time on my hands I would like to find a way to be useful to the community.

I am in charge of my medical decisions, but we have all the paperwork drawn up for Master to act as my Medical Power of Attorney should that need arise. I would trust him completely to act in my best interests. I can't stress the importance of this kind of paperwork. If you don't have your papers in order, get them in order immediately.

My advice for a Dominant considering a disabled s-type or one that suddenly has a disabled s-type is what I've actually learned from how my Master has handled the changes in our relationship. He collared me, all of me—good, bad and the ugly—and I'm much more than the sum of my parts, working or not. Remember that, and you can make it through.

Finding Your Value

slave ziggy

I'm a 48-year-old male-identified slave, in the service of my Mistress. I began my journey into BDSM in the fetish clubs of Japan in 1982 while serving in the Marines. Upon returning to the U.S., I found my way to various leather bars and clubs around the US.. Everywhere I was stationed, I was able to find Leatherfolk.

For many years I concentrated on learning what it meant to be an experienced and skilled bottom. I had a great time challenging myself to conquer various fears, and I was fortunate to have opportunities to serve a variety of individuals. Through the guidance of knowledgeable and skilled tops and the example of my slave brothers, I discovered my desire to surrender. I had engaged in a few dominant and submissive relationships, but it wasn't until I connected with my first owner that I realized what was alive and true for me.

While serving in the Marines in 1987, I was involved in a motor vehicle accident that required advance lifesaving measures. I was injured when a mortar round fell short of it intended target killing the driver and seven out of the nine men in the back. I sustained a spinal cord injury, along with a head injury which left me unable to walk. When I awoke, I had little or no feeling from about the middle of my chest on down. Fortunately, after nearly two years of rehab, I am able to walk, although I still have some residual issues as a result of my injuries. I am able to function fairly well, but I am not as strong as I was back then, and I experience chronic pain and weakness in my legs. The weirdest thing is that the head injury left me with what is best described as vision issues. No, I am not blind, and for the most part see just fine, but I have a lot of visual problems—for example, I can't see the spaces between the words. Funny for someone who aspires to be a writer, right? (Physical problems are not the only effects of serving in the military and being exposed to difficult situations; for years I have also dealt with Post Traumatic Stress Disorder.)

I had been a slave before my accident, and I didn't feel as if the accident had very much to do with how I felt about that identity. However, it did force me to focus on being healthy enough to service and surrender in ways that would be fulfilling for myself and a master. The plus side of my accident was that there was no denying my challenges. This meant I had to be open and honest about my physical limitations—after all, I looked fine on the outside. If there was any other positive thing to come of being so banged up, it would have to be the change in how I see things. It could have been a lot worse, after all; I might very well have not been here to answer these questions. I think when something like this happens, it forces you to look at what you can do rather than what you can't. It creates value where some would not see it. If *I* don't believe in who I am or what I can offer, no one else will; it is seeing what we bring to the relationship that makes us the most able.

I have been in my current relationship for 10 years. We are Master and slave in a situation where service, obedience and control are the central focus. I came to the relationship disabled, but Mistress dealt with it very well. She set up protocols and directives just as any other master would, but she took my abilities into account. I attribute this to our basic compatibility. She requires me to strive for excellence and do my very best. However, she does not require service or surrender outside my abilities. Things have pretty much remained constant since we have been together, although I am sure that if my condition worsens over time, more things may change. I imagine that things will change anyway as we both age.

My owner and I both have a realistic view of our skills and abilities. I think the key is communicating openly and honestly on a daily basis. If I am physically unable to do something, I communicate that to Mistress and she makes the necessary adjustments. There is no shame in not being able to do something. There is only doing my level best to be of service. Mistress' number one rule is for me to take care of her property.

On the other hand, I think the key to Mistress and I having a fulfilling relationship has been about fully understanding my physical limitations, setting both of us up for success. She does challenge and encourage me to be a better person and a better slave, and she is ever mindful of creating opportunities for me to express my surrender both physically and emotionally, despite any physical limitation I may have.

I handle all of my own medical decisions. I may consult with Mistress if I'm struggling with something, but otherwise it is important to us both that I retain my ability to be my own medical advocate and make choices that are in my best interest. This is not to say that Mistress' opinion is excluded, but it does mean that she trusts me to take care of myself. I believe that it is healthy for slaves to retain this type of personal power. I can't expect that Mistress is going to take on everything, and as long as I am able to do so, I will. In the event that I become unable to make such choices, Mistress has the ability and the responsibility to do so. In ten years we have never argued over any medical decisions I have had to make.

Mistress has been extremely supportive of my pursuit of alternative medicines, and has also encouraged me to follow my passions and enjoy the activities that fulfill me and that I am able to do. She acknowledges that although I am her slave, there is more to me than just what I can do for her.

Before the accident, I was at the peak of my fitness. I ran, biked, and often participated in triathlons. I had also already been involved in SM for about 4 years when it happened. Strangely, I didn't see myself as being excluded from SM or service; I simply needed to shift my attention and energy towards healing.

When I think about it today, it is amazing that I even survived when eight other Marines didn't. As you can imagine, there is a lot baggage that comes from surviving something like that. It's a sort of bittersweet. I have been haunted by that fact for years. It's true what they say about how the physical injuries tend to heal much faster than the emotional ones. It is also true that trauma does change our brain chemistry, and that too must be acknowledged and dealt with. I don't believe those experiences ever fully leave us.

Although the U.S. has made great strides in laws pertaining to accessibility and fair hiring practices, the road to understanding hidden disabilities is still a long and arduous endeavor. Many people still feel that if your disabilities cannot be seen, then your shortcomings must be a matter of you just not making the effort. The fact that the power exchange demographic is a microcosm of the greater society means that it is more likely than not that there are many people with hidden disabilities, and there are an equal number of folks that just simply don't understand. I've found, in my travels and in talking with people in my power exchange community, that gaining a better understanding of these internal challenges is critical in order for both partners to find compatibility and fulfillment. I've never been the activist sort, but my focus in community is to aid others in understanding themselves, and help them to fulfill their desires to be either master or slave.

Whether we like it or not, I guess most of us come to the Master/slave dynamic with a perception of who we should be as slaves. Even though I would consider myself no stranger to power exchange relationships, I too catch myself looking for validation of my identity; I believe that it is human nature to do so. However, it is the amount of weight we place on other people's view of our identity that can become an issue.

I believe in order for us as slaves to find what we are looking for, it must begin with understanding how we perceive ourselves. It is easier to assess our deficits than to acknowledge the positive qualities we bring to the table. Studies have shown that people with physical and emotional challenges tend to value things in different ways when assessing the quality of their lives. The usual assumption is that if you have challenges, you have a lower perception of your quality of life. However, studies done at Brigham Young University in 2007 have shown this is not true; out of nearly 13,000 participants, those who had a reportable disability tended to have a higher perception of the quality of life. In addition, they tended to place a higher value on friends, family, relationships and community than those with no reportable disabilities.

I have found that accepting and adapting to any physical or emotional challenge begins with assessing what you have to work with. The work of the individual is finding value in themselves. The goal is to raise your level of well-being. This can be done in a number of ways. For example, I can't participate in triathlons now, so I have discovered an interest in repairing and restoring bicycles. It's a far cry from the thrill and drive to compete and test the limits of my body, but it does bring me a great deal of satisfaction: to take something that someone has given up on and create a thing of use. It is a powerful metaphor for someone who once couldn't walk.

Finding your value is something we often mistake for boastfulness or ego gone awry, but in fact when we choose to focus on the abilities and values we have, we are able to better deal with our challenges. It also allows us the brain space to see how we can work around those challenges and lead a more fulfilling life—although I acknowledge for all of us with challenges there are stages we go through. In some ways it is akin to the grieving process. Just as with grieving, the people closest to us need to not expect us to be any more or any less than where we are.

The advice I would give others who struggle with physical and emotional challenges is to remember that 80 percent of being a slave is how you think and 20 percent of being a slave is what you do. Having said that, it is also important to remember that you are the expert on your challenges, which means you are responsible for sharing as much as possible with a potential owner. Your owner is there to support any therapeutic process which improves your condition, but you share the greater portion of the responsibility for your health and welfare.

The role of our dominant partners should always be one of support and encouragement. Their ability to know when to be challenging and when to be encouraging depends greatly on our ability to effectively communicate where we are at any given time. It also means we must have insight as to our particular and unique challenge. It is safe to say that my challenges may seem the same as those of many other people, but how they manifest may be significantly different. Even if your master has experience with disabilities, never assume they get your particular challenge. Also, it goes without saying that masters are not mind readers. Many common misconceptions can be alleviated through our ability to communicate with others effectively. I acknowledge, however, that sometimes this can be difficult.

So much of how we view our value is wrapped up in what we believe we are able to do. The root of this comes from fear of rejection, or of being devalued. As hard as it might be, we are often called upon to call up courage as a way of dealing with our fears. Those fears are further compounded by looking at others and attempting to model or mimic what we see in them. I think and say that I wish I could be more like other slaves, but I am not them, and the more I tried to be someone I was not, the harder it became. It was not until I let go of what I perceived as the "perfect slave" that I was able to see my own value.

Communication is key in all types of relationships. including Master/slave. However, what is less discussed is the way we communicate with ourselves. Even if we have already assessed our value and quality of life, how we talk to ourselves greatly affects the quality of our relationships and our interactions in the greater community. Negative self-talk only serves as a roadblock to achieving our desired goals; it misdirects our energy. Bear in mind that I do believe it can be helpful to assess our service and surrender as a way to gain understanding and open the door of improvement. However, doing this with a gentle and encouraging inner voice can mean the difference between being fulfilled in your service and developing an impossible scenario.

About twelve years ago I met a couple who had been together about five years; they were married and seemed to be doing very well. One day Mistress and I were at a munch when my friend—the slave—came in. I noticed right away that she was not wearing her collar. When I inquired, she whispered that she had been released. We talked later, and she revealed that she could no longer kneel and get into the positions indicative of a Gorean slave. Admittedly, my first instinct was to cry. Then I got mad, and from there I tried to understand the master's point.

Despite my friend's distress, I guess I can try to look beyond my own feelings to understand he simply wanted a slave that could do all the things he perceived as important. To him, his slave was nothing more than utilitarian property, and his property was worn out, and it was time to get another. However, for those of us who are seen by our partners as more than just property, it felt as though he had lost sight of the big picture. We all age, and we are all eventually met with some challenge or another. In this case, the slave's ability to kneel was irrelevant to what the act of kneeling really means.

The position of kneeling is about the outward expression of surrender, of deference to the master. In looking at this from a practical perspective, what would be the difference in kneeling versus sitting on a cushion or kneeling bench? The slave is in front or beside the master, and is lower and easily accessible. Regardless, if the master's role is to provide the slave opportunities to surrender their will both physically and emotionally, then it is important to make necessary adjustments to achieve surrender. These should all be part of the dynamic. (By the way, several months later she found a master who was willing to look past her physical limitations and create a dynamic that was fulfilling to both of them.)

I think that we often see service only as its physical expression—what we can physically do for our masters. To me, service is multidimensional. This means that there are still things I can do even if I am having a bad day. If I am truly unable to do anything that day, Mistress is willing to assist me when I need it. This is good for both of us. I want to be able to serve her fully, but the days I am unable to provide my usual service are opportunities for Mistress to get to exercise some skills and abilities she may not find a reason to do on a regular basis. It also prevents me from owning the service I provide, which is an important point.

Lastly—and sometimes the most difficult—is being more than just our disabilities. Dealing with our challenges can sometimes seem like a full time job, and just as with work, we all need a break. This is not to say that we are able to take off our disabilities and hang them in a closet for the night. It is to say that even when it is at its hardest, our ability to be more than our disabilities is critical. All humans are multifaceted and we take on a plethora of identities throughout our lifetimes. The identity of "slave" may act as a sort of umbrella for other identities, but at the end of the day, I am more than just a slave. The same can be said about our challenges; I am not just my challenges. Wise and compatible masters get this, and look for ways to help us work around our challenges while getting what we need in surrender. Our job is to look for opportunities work around our problems, and to adapt to changes as they arise.

We must find the courage to stand in the face of fear in order that we might live a life of fulfillment beyond measure.

M/s With MS
slave carla

Fifteen years ago, I came home from the doctor's office with bad news for my Master. I'm forty-six years old, and at the time I'd only been his slave for a couple of years. We were new to M/s, and still trying to find our way, but I'd been getting more and more sick since before I'd met him. He knew that I had some kind of chronic illness, but we'd both been frightened by seeing how much it had progressed in the past year. Finally he ordered me to give up and go to the doctors, because my attempts at home cures weren't working. They diagnosed me with multiple sclerosis, and trigeminal neuralgia caused by the MS. Later, I would also be diagnosed with a seizure disorder and put on still more medications.

I had two kids (and three dogs and four cats) from a previous marriage, and no contact with or help from my children's father, so everything had fallen on me for the last decade. I worked a full-time, highly stressful job, and then came home and took care of everyone. I was SuperMom, SuperWife, and I tried hard to be SuperSlave when K and I got together. Then the illness struck, and my life cascaded to a halt.

After my diagnosis, we backed off on the M/s for a little while. I think that K, my husband and Master, wanted to give me space to adapt to the idea of being disabled. I also think that he didn't know what to do with me, and he needed his own chance to mourn the life that could have been. I quit my job, went on disability, and crawled into a cocoon of pain for about six months. At the end of it, I crawled out again and said to him, "I may be a broken slave, but can I at least be your slave again, if only a little?" We talked about it for the next month, and then he re-collared me. The second collaring was very different from the idealistic first one. We were quieter and more serious, and we understood that what we were doing was going to be a big undertaking. Neither of us knew what it was going to mean, taking me on as a slave when I was in this state.

First, I had to relearn how to use my broken body. That was hard, because what I wanted to do more than anything was to just ignore it entirely, but that was the absolute wrong thing to do. I had to pay attention to its signals so that I could learn to gauge my ability to function at any time, when I needed medication, when I needed to rest, and when I knew that I only had another half an hour in me. Paying attention to a body that just gives out pain and fatigue, a body that has made me feel betrayed, was so hard that sometimes I would just lie in bed and cry. Master helped by sitting next to me, being comforting, and then making me tell him everything about how I felt physically. Slowly, over time, I learned to give him that report whenever he asked for it, and then to give it to myself.

One of the hardest things that I learned to do was to speak up when I was feeling too awful. I can take a lot of pain (which made me a great bottom) and I'm used to being everyone's caretaker, but I had to admit to myself that I couldn't do everything any more. I had to learn to take care of myself first, or I wouldn't be able to take care of anyone else. Learning to say, "I can't hang the laundry today, would you please do that for me?" was excruciatingly difficult. However, K's first rule for me is to protect the property, and if I run the property into the ground, that's disrespecting his orders. I find it a lot easier to respect and take care of my body if I know that it's really taking care of something that he loves, values ... and owns.

A slave who has a disability that involves pain and/or fatigue has a greater responsibility to be honest, both with her Master and with herself. It's easy, on the bad days, to use the illness as an excuse to get out of doing things you don't want to do. For other slaves, it may be even easier to ignore the warning signs and push themselves past the breaking point. But lying to K about my current state of health is not only wrong, it's also unfair to him because it makes his job so much harder and sets him up to fail. This means that I have to think hard about my condition each day, and try to let him know what he has to work with.

These days I've learned to be constantly checking in with my body. I get up, I stretch, I see where my range of motion might be, I check how tired I am just getting to the toilet. Since I have to go to the toilet about ten times more often than I used to before MS (more on that later!) I have plenty of time to gauge things. Every time I try to go up and down stairs, I check to see how my legs are doing. Some days there's no doing stairs. Some days there's no walking, even, and I have my little electric scooter to get around. Each time I notice a symptom, I mentally "clock" it on a scale in my head so that I can report to him. My master works from home so that he can be there for me when needed, and I check in with him in the morning, during his afternoon lunch break, and in the evening before making dinner. At each check-in, he decides what my chores will be based on what I tell him about my symptoms. It's a matter of trust— he trusts me to be honest about what I can handle, and I trust him to take my reports seriously.

I think that my kids had it the hardest, because they were used to SuperMom, and it was difficult for them to understand why Mom couldn't play basketball with them anymore, or why I couldn't get out of bed on some days. I've found that the spoon theory is one of the best tools ever for explaining a chronic illness to friends and family. My kids ask about my spoons, and have become pretty decent at calibrating them—"Mom, you should sit down, you don't need to waste a spoon on that." I've learned to plan out my day, carefully hoarding my spoons, to get the most out of each one.

My master and I work things a week at a time. On Sunday night, we'll talk about what has to be done for the week, and we'll prioritize it. I'll try my best to get to each item as I have the spoons to do it. If we tried to manage things by the day, there would be whole days where nothing would get done. This means that he often doesn't get things exactly when he wants them, but he pointed out that honestly, there's nothing that I do for him that he isn't capable of doing for himself—after all, he is a capable adult—and if he wants something that badly right now, he can do it himself. On our weekly schedule, the rule is that if Thursday night comes along and I'm lagging way behind, I have to come to him and tell him that it's a bad week, and I'm not going to be able to accomplish everything. He looks at the list and pulls things off of it, changes the priorities until they are more manageable, and then I work to get the new shortened list done by Sunday. Anything not done is carried over. Obviously some things have deadlines (and I try to do them first), but he knows that it's good for my self-esteem to be able to do whatever I can; I just have trouble prioritizing, so that's his job. It's important to him that things get done, but not when or how.

Little protocols have become very important to us. I can't kneel (that's why I laughed so much when I saw that the title of this book was going to be *Kneeling In Spirit*) but it doesn't hurt me to wait to eat until he starts eating, or wear what clothes he tells me to wear, or any number of other small things that the kids won't notice and that I can do all the time. If I can make it to the table, I can wait until he takes his first bite to pick up my fork. If I can make it out of bed and dress, I can wear what he likes. If I can manage to make dinner occasionally, I can make what he likes, or what he thinks I ought to be eating in order to keep me healthier.

Some of the most humiliating symptoms of MS are the loss of bladder control from the bladder nerves going spastic, and loss of bowel control. Sometimes my bladder demands to be emptied so frequently I can't get to the bathroom in time. Sometimes I can't even feel it when it runs out of me. Sometimes it doesn't all manage to come out, and I developed a bladder infection a few times. I'm on medications for it, which helps, but it's still a daily battle. After the first bladder infection, my doctor tried to get me to learn to put in a catheter in order to get all the urine out, which does help me go longer between bathroom visits and I dribble less. I couldn't do it. I just couldn't seem to make myself put it in, and my hands shook, and I cried. I cried again later on Master's shoulder, and he said, "Let's take a look at that thing."

The next I knew, I was naked and spread-eagled on the bed with him kneeling between my legs squinting at my urethra, and then he'd gotten the catheter into me with one swift move and I was pissing into a pan on the bedroom floor. It felt weird, but since I was relaxed, it wasn't nearly as uncomfortable as when I tried to do it myself. After we were done, he carefully pulled the cath out, wiped me down with my special wipes, and then he pulled his hard-on out of his pants and fucked me good. I totally wasn't expecting it. "I'll be doing that for you from now on," he told me, and ever since then he's catheterized me once or twice daily (although we don't always have sex afterwards). I've learned to do it myself on the days when he's away, but I still prefer being turned upside down, spread wide, tubed up by him, and made to piss in a pan on the floor. (After all, I am a submissive!) Sometimes he has me do it on all fours, squatting over the pan like a dog. (I can't get down and up from the floor, so he has to put me there and pick me up.)

When we go out, he sometimes makes me wear diapers which he'll put on me himself, and he'll make the occasional private comment about it that makes me blush. Sometimes I dribble when we have sex; if he doesn't want that to happen he'll cath me first, but he's also fucked me over the edge of the bathtub, propped with rolled towels, while I pissed. "Fucked the piss out of you," he said. All this may make some people cringe, but it's a way we've reframed what would otherwise be a bad humiliation into a good one. It puts some kink back into the situation, so neither of us feels like my disability is getting in the way of our kinky sex life. Before the MS got bad, we were never into controlling my bodily functions—I didn't ask permission to pee or anything—but now this has given us a new chance to explore this area of control, and he is surprised by how much he likes it.

My bowels are also a problem. I am prone to constipation when the nerves don't tell my bowels to move fast enough, and prone to diarrhea when they move too fast. He's learned how to give me suppositories or enemas when either of these problems arise. Sometimes when it won't come out, he'll just glove up and finger me there, and then the nerves get stimulated and I can go. He likes giving me the enemas because it involves putting my ass in the air, violating it with more tubes, and flushing me out. Then I'm nice and clean for anal sex if he wants it. Once he took a photo of me—or my ass, anyway—with the enema tube up my ass and the bag hanging above me, the cath in my urethra while I pissed into a pan below me, and a little vibrator stuffed into my cunt between them. He posted it online somewhere, but you'll never find it—and if you do, you'd never know that the woman in that picture spends a third of her time in a wheelchair.

Sex itself is a little difficult because the nerves in my genitals don't always work, and I don't produce much lubrication anymore, so I have to use a lot of lube. There's also that I'm often tired or in pain, but even then we've figured out entirely passive things I can offer—like him using my breasts to fuck and get off. I am enough of a slave in my heart that I take a good deal of pleasure in him just using me, even when I can't get my own nerve endings to cooperate. Using a vibrator helps "prime the pump" and sometimes he'll make me sit on one while I'm in my chair. I get leg spasms at times, and it can be hard for me to keep my legs spread apart ... but that's what bondage is for, right? If you're a kinkster crip, anyway.

My Master also gives me my nightly injections of medication—he says that it's just one more way that he penetrates me, and he jokes about it being "needle play". I also sometimes get uncontrollable episodes of laughing or crying that don't have anything to do with what's actually happening—they're just the MS attacking my brain; it's called the "pseudobulbar effect". We've found that the best thing to stop them is just to have him grab me by the hair and slap me a few times, hard. It sounds crazy, and it might not work for everyone with this problem, but it seems to do something to my neurology that shuts the episode right up.

I have trouble with heat, so we turned the spare bedroom into the "cold room", heavily air conditioned, where I can retreat periodically when I get overheated. The kids are not allowed in, and I also use it for lying down during the day when I need to rest. The rule is that I have to be naked in there—the "cool room" is the place where his naked slave is stored—and I fasten my ankles to the bed with soft restraints while I rest, to remember that I'm owned. A poem I found that reminds me about being a good slave is pasted to the ceiling above me. So it's not just a medical retreat but a way to remember who and what I am as well.

Probably the best thing that Master has done is that he has taken control of my medical decisions. That was a difficult decision for me, not because I didn't want him to do it—actually, I desperately wanted out of making those decisions—but because I thought that I'd be a failure as a human being if I didn't take care of that myself. Even some other sub friends had told me that I'd be copping out somehow to let him take over completely. But Master read up on MS—he probably knows more about it than I do—and he started coming to doctor appointments with me, ostensibly to help me remember what was said. Finally one day I was faced with a decision about a certain medication and its side effects, and I just couldn't make it. I sat there and cried for hours, I had no idea what to do. Master came in and held me, and then, of course, he mentioned his opinions on the subject. He had plenty, and they were well thought through. All I could think of was how much I trusted his judgment on a daily basis anyway. He is a sensible and thoughtful man, and since I was already trusting him on so many other things, why not this? I begged him to make the decision, and I begged him to just make all the medical decisions for me from now on.

He said that he'd be willing to do that, but that he was human and might make mistakes. He told me that if I wanted him to take control, I couldn't blame him and give him trouble when he didn't decide perfectly. After all, if I was giving that up, it was my choice and I'd have to live with it. He also said that I didn't get to argue with him, because that was undermining to him, and he might as well not be doing it. If I wanted the right to argue, I could make my own decisions.

I told him that his mistakes couldn't possibly be any worse than mine, and so it was done. For the last few years he's made all the decisions about any course of treatment. He listens to the doctors, reads up on the treatments, tells me what I'm going to do, and I go in and request it. So far it's worked out great. Just coping with this disease is all I can do sometimes; having the decision-making process taken off my shoulders is a huge relief for me, and an act of trust in our relationship. It's not a copout, it's one of the ways that I feel my slavehood, and one of the ways that he, as my master, protects me from one small part of the difficulties of my life.

He can't protect me from MS, but he can take that burden away from me, and I'm grateful.

We're taking it one day at a time. I know that this disease will progress, and eventually I may end up completely bedridden, but we're going to do everything we can to stave off that day. I hope that even when I can't get out of bed, I can still offer my wonderful Master some kind of satisfaction in my surrender, my trust, and the complete devotion of my heart.

Out Of Sight

slave reji

I don't ever remember having decent vision. From childhood, I was the kid with the thick glasses, and then in my teens even thick glasses didn't help as much. By the time I was 20, it was clear that I was probably going to end mostly or even completely blind eventually.

I have a genetic eye disorder that is progressive and currently not very treatable. Medical science is working on it—or so they tell me—but I'll probably be dead before any breakthroughs make it to my eyes. In a way, I was lucky—I knew that it was coming, and I had time to prepare. I've got a friend who lost his vision suddenly, through a brain trauma, and was completely unprepared for a life lived in darkness. So it could have been much worse.

I'm not actually living in darkness at this time, however. I have some blurred peripheral vision; I can see colors, large hand motions, light and darkness, some vague shapes. I've lost most of my ability to read over the past decade; I can make out very large letters with a magnifying glass, but it's so tedious as to not be worth the bother most of the time. I can't drive—obviously—but that doesn't mean that I'm helpless and can't work. I'd better be able to work—I'm a slave! Not that Aline, my Mistress, would throw me out on my ear if I was run over by a truck tomorrow and was crippled as well as blind, but it has been wonderful to find ways to serve her even without eyes.

In school, I was self-conscious about my vision impairment and my subsequent difficulty with studies. I turned to athletics—I could see well enough to run around a track, although flying balls were a problem. I did every sport and fitness activity I could find that didn't involve flying objects, from gymnastics to weightlifting. Since I was also a girl who wasn't terribly feminine, becoming a jock was a place I could shine. If I was going to be mocked for being too butch, I might as well make something of it. Athletics also made me feel strong in the face of the helplessness I felt from my degenerating vision. And yes, I got called a dyke, even before I understood what that meant.

Actually, I got crushes on both boys and girls. I would attach myself to some bright, charismatic person as if they were a lamp that could warm me. I'd do anything to help them—carry their heavy stuff (I was strong for a girl), run errands, be a companion. I desperately wanted to be allowed to do good things for them, and see them made happy through my efforts. I didn't have the word *service* to describe what I was doing at the time. Service was something that people got paid to do. This was done out of love, or admiration, or some puppy-like combination of the two. In hindsight, I can see how many people took advantage of me and then tossed me aside, the awkward androgynous girl-jock with the thick glasses. I rendered sexual service too— my first three sexual experiences were me saying, "What would you want me to do that would make you happy?" The boys would take it, but tell me that we "weren't dating—this was just casual," while the girls would order me not to tell anyone about it, on pain of total social rejection.

My sexual fantasies at this point were riddled with scenarios about braving the evil wizard's castle in order to rescue the fair maiden (or prince, like I said, I wasn't picky about that), and of course I would be caught and given the chance to be tortured in their stead ... and of course I would accept. I'm not sure whether I simply learned to eroticize suffering for others through sexual fantasy, or whether that was already present in my subconscious and creeping out during sexual longings. I do remember being seventeen and doing a marathon cunnilingus session with one of those girls who wouldn't acknowledge me afterward. My pants stayed on, not because I was stone or anything, but because she wasn't interested in doing anything to me except sort of patting my head occasionally. I gave her something like ten orgasms, and I realized guiltily halfway through that I was getting off on being used without any thought for my own pleasure.

I would run around in circles in my head over that. There was a weird pleasure in it, yet I did actually want someone who would desire and care about me. Had I just eroticized being unwanted and unloved, a sexual machine to use and cast aside? I sometimes worry that I might have ended up in a pretty bad place if I hadn't run across the right people.

My first master was J, another butch woman. She taught me what to look for in someone to serve—honor, maturity, common sense—and in fact she taught me the meaning of service. The real meaning. I learned that it was something to be proud of, something that could be perfected. She also taught me that my urge to sexual suffering could be put to good use by a sadist. Our second date was at a play party, and I wandered around listening to all the noises, my eyes bugging out behind my thick glasses. It was my evil wizard's dungeon fantasy come true, only the evil wizard and the hero were one and the same. When I got strung up and whipped, it felt like coming home.

I loved J desperately, mutely, doggedly, somewhere between the way a groupie loves a rock star and a little boy loves their war-hero older brother. I'd imprinted on her like a duckling. I was terrified that she would eventually reject me because I was going blind, but she didn't—she rejected me because I wasn't feminine enough. I'd been an exception for her, and after a while she could see that it wasn't going to work out. I was crushed. I was even more sensitive about my discomfort with being feminine than I was about my vision. I didn't think that anything could hurt worse than being rejected for a disability until I was rejected for being, well, sort of butch but not butch enough or femme enough ... by another butch. I was neither fish nor fowl, it seemed, and I wasn't enough to stir her desire.

We went to one last play party after our final argument, but J didn't play with me. Instead, she handed me off to a friend to play with, a woman I didn't even know. I was furious with her, and certain that the scene would be terrible, but it was wonderful in a weird way. I cried all the way through it. The gorgeous full-figured dark-haired dyke with the white Irish skin didn't bat an eye. She just hurt me, and let me cry, and crooned, "Yes, honey, cry it all out," and then hurt me some more. I was not the first bottom who'd cried out their breakup under her whip, and I wasn't the first one who had come home with her that night, either. But apparently I'm the first one who ever stayed.

Her name was—is—Aline, and she collared me after a few months. We have been together for six years now. It wasn't a case of being desperate and taking the first thing that came along—J later told me that she'd been sure that Aline and I would suit each other well, and she was right. Where J was a rock star, Aline was a lover. She crawled into my head and pulled out all the insecurities, and put each one to sleep with a magic hand. She was the first person to get me off, and then to make me come again and again until I screamed for mercy.

She was also the first person to tell me that she liked my gender presentation. I wasn't just an unwomanly nerd-jock, I was an "intellectual butch" with muscles she could admire. When she touched me, I felt handsome for the first time. I'd been hung up on the fact that I'd never be beautiful, and suddenly I was handsome. (Yeah, there's a difference. So there.)

I moved in right after she collared me, and we immediately had the problem of Where To Put Things. It's important to me that there is a place for everything in the house, and that everything is in its place. It's not about neatness, it's simple self-defense—I lose items easily when I can't see them, and looking for anything that has gotten lost is so hard that it sometimes makes me panic. I don't mind being the person to put things away, but I have a hard time finding all the various debris in a cluttered, scattered house. I also tend to trip over items that aren't on furniture. Even though she is my mistress, Aline made a huge sacrifice in reordering her house and learning to be neater instead of the messy person she is more naturally. She claims that it wasn't a sacrifice because she's now got a permanent house-cleaner, but I saw how difficult it was for her in the beginning. I was afraid that she wouldn't want me because I was so much trouble, but she held on to me anyway.

It wasn't that my blindness was never an issue. She knew what she was getting into with me, and she'd actually had a blind lover for a brief time beforehand, although she hadn't lived with him. She was aware that I would only get worse. The problem was that she thought I could be handling the onslaught with a better and more practical attitude. I'd been used to dealing with it all by myself—not making a big deal about it, trying to make it intrude as little as possible into my partners' lives. Aline was the first person I lived with, and the first full-time owner, and she was having none of that.

For example, eye strain is a big problem for me—in order to make use of the little bit of vision I have left, I have to strain to focus, and sometimes that results in awful headaches. Aline and I had our first big argument over that. She felt that it was better for me to spend a certain amount of time each day without vision at all, relaxing what was left of my eyes, than to have awful headaches that make me irritable. (As she was the one who would have to put up with the irritability, I could see how that would be important to her.) To me, that was giving in to the onslaught of the illness. It was admitting that I was just blind instead of struggling against it. Aline pointed out that I was probably going to end up totally blind anyway, and I ought to spend some time adjusting to it. I argued that there would be plenty of time for me to adjust when there was no other choice, and I wanted to enjoy my vision while I had it. She got out a blindfold, put it on me, and ordered me to stay that way for the next four hours. She won.

During that four hours, my assignment was to go about my daily tasks and make notes—on a little voice recorder— about how hard or easy they had become without any vision. Then, she said, we could sit down and talk about how to make them easier. Technology has come up with a variety of interesting tools to help the visually impaired; I'd just been resisting them because they made me face how disabled I'd become. After spending part of each day forcibly in darkness, I was a lot less resistant to getting one of those vegetable choppers that consists of a plastic cylinder with a spring-blade in the middle, and actually using it—not to mention all the other possibilities I'd been avoiding. (This essay, for example, has been written with dictation software. I needed to give up and accept my blindness before I could bring myself to work with it.)

I won't say it was easy, because it wasn't. The third day spent with the afternoon in darkness, I broke down and cried. Aline was right there—I hadn't noticed that she'd been in sight of me the whole time, keeping an eye on me—and she comforted me. She didn't take the blindfold off, even though

I begged her to, but she did take me into bed with her right then, and reminded me that I didn't need eyes to service her in the way we both loved the most.

Sometimes it's felt like Aline's managing of my condition makes me weak. I need to feel strong in some ways—I still work out and run, I don't need great vision to stay on a path through the park, I can still carry all the bags—and being the strong silent one who never let on about my troubles was part of that. Except that she sees I'm doing it, and calls me on it. "Don't be a martyr!" she says. "Don't waste your talent for enduring suffering on stupid stuff we can compensate for! Save it for the things we can't change!" If I don't do something about it, she'll step in and take care of it. I swore service and surrender to her, so I have to bow my head and go along with it. Our agreement states that if I honestly believe that her efforts will do me harm, I have to stop her. So far, though, I've never had to do that. Usually I know that she's right, and I'm just being a stubborn idiot, and it's not going to do me harm to stop being a stubborn idiot.

There are a hundred ways in which she helps me to gracefully manage my condition, and she doesn't let me feel bad about that. When I get into a self-flagellating mood, she just tells me that I'm a better slave to her when I'm able to do my work smoothly, and that's worth it to her. For instance, she often wears bells or jingly things when we are out in a crowd, like a leather or GLBT event. She got some comments about how bells are slave things (which is ridiculous) so I bought her jingly spurs to wear on her boots. That way I can find her if I lose her in a crowd, and I can hear her coming down a hallway. If people are approaching us, she tells me who they are, since I can't see facial details. At play parties, I'm usually always leashed to her, which helps. She buys me books on tape, tells me about visual details in movies, and is always on the lookout for new devices to help me in my daily tasks.

Most important of all, she refuses to let me be either a whiner or a martyr. She expects me to do what I can, and to admit when I can't do something. When I'm trying to pretend that I can do an activity that is actually really risky for me, that makes me less reliable, and I risk disappointing her and letting her down. She's insisted that I keep my job as a tech support phone person, because she knows that being able to bring her a paycheck gives me some self-esteem. I trust her to have my best interests at heart, and when I'm not all emotionally snarled up in knots, I enjoy being able to sail along in her wake and let her make the decisions.

I'm not a slave because my lack of vision makes me helpless. I'm a slave because I love to be helpful, and because I have surrendered to a wonderful woman. Finding the right person to hold my leash and help me to serve them in the best way possible has been a kind of freedom. I am confident that we can feel our way, together, through whatever the future brings.

Geisha On Wheels

kitsu

On the wall next to my computer is a little cartoon of a toy geisha on a wooden stand with wheels, with a pull-string. She is holding out a bento box full of food, and she has a smile on her face. My master found it online and sent it to me, saying, "This is you—a geisha on wheels." It's been our private joke ever since.

I'm not Japanese, but I read up a little on the geisha. While they were essentially courtesans—high-class prostitutes—they were expected to do more than suck cock and lie around to get fucked. The word means "artist", and they were expected to give excellent companionship as well as excellent sex. A geisha was well-read and could discuss many subjects from poetry to politics. She could arrange flowers and decorate a room. She could sing, play a musical instrument, and perhaps orate. She could accompany him to an event and share in his interest and enthusiasm. She could play the hostess and make a whole group of people feel welcomed. She could shine her spotlight of attention on a man and make him feel like the most special person in the world.

That's what I do for my Sir. I'm not an owned slave—I identify as his submissive and I don't live with him, because I need my own accessible apartment—but I can do everything I just described, and it doesn't matter that I can't do it walking. My job is to make sure that in my own private island of the world, he gets what he wants as much as is humanly possible. I am dedicated to making him happy. Serving him fulfills and completes me. Seeing him light up when he lets himself into my apartment and sees me waiting for him, that's the best gift I could be given.

I don't wait for him on my knees, because I can't get on the floor without a great deal of help. He doesn't mind, and tells me so. What he wants is my complete attention, not a specific position or act. That said, my Sir is really into breasts, and I'm lucky that I have a nice rack, or so he says. He's also into the fact that when I'm sitting in my chair, I'm at a good level to either suck his cock or take it between my tits. My breasts are very sensitive, and they are the major way I get off, since I don't have feeling in my lower half.

When I was eight, I was in a car accident that killed two of the other kids in the heavily loaded station wagon, driven by a harried Girl Scout assistant leader. To this day I don't know exactly what happened, except that we were all being raucous in the back seats, and then there was a crash and I blacked out. When I woke up, I was covered in casts and in traction, paralyzed from the waist down. It took me months of rehab just to be able to feed myself. I lost a year of school, but I made it up and graduated on time with my class, years later. I've never let being a para stop me from doing whatever I wanted ... even being a geisha.

When I was in my teens, I read a fictional autobiography of Queen Eleanor of Aquitaine. I read a lot of biographies of strong women, mostly because I was trying to buck myself up and assert myself to people who infantilize and ignore crips in wheelchairs. "See, you're strong, just like Queen Elizabeth I, you can roll up and talk to that mean-looking store clerk!" Anyway, the novel. There was a point where the independent and controlling Queen finds out that her powerful husband, Henry II, is having an affair with some minor nobleman's daughter. She's been his lover for years now, and the Queen never knew. In the novel, the Queen goes to see the young woman, whose name is Rosamund Clifford. She expects to find another strong, controlling woman who is scheming to take the Queen's place. Instead, she finds a sweet, kind girl who dotes on the King. She doesn't argue politics with him, or fight with him. The Queen asks what they talk about, trying to find out what is so fascinating about Rosamund. The King's mistress says simply that he talks about whatever he wants, and she strokes his hair and says, "There, there." She doesn't often understand what he's going on about, but she is always a good listener, and is determined to be an island of calm and happiness in his difficult life.

I knew that I was supposed to identify with strong Eleanor, but something in me stirred and sighed at the thought of being Rosamund. I was shocked at myself, and I pushed it down—how could I sit here fantasizing about living for some man's attention, being a passive cup for him to fill and drink from, and then see him off into the night until the next time he deigned to arrive? Wasn't that horribly codependent? The Rosamund fantasy was to wait for some years, until I was much older and had a career and an accessible condo. I only dated very submissive men—not in a BDSM sense but just men with submissive personalities—I think because I wasn't ready to be submissive myself, and I knew that a more dominant man would make me melt. I didn't want to melt for just anyone, though. I was also very suspicious of any man who would approach me, because I assumed that no man would want a para unless they were some kind of fetishist.

I met my Sir at a BDSM munch, which I went to reluctantly with a friend. My reluctance was partially about my love-hate relationship with wanting to submit sexually, and partly about the fact that the food court in the mall had steps and no ramp, so I had to find friends to get me up and down to the tables. My Sir hadn't arrived yet, and he missed that debacle. Grumpy, I parked myself behind a table with a wall of planters at my back, and eventually drowned my sorrows in conversation with friends. He arrived, sat at our table, and suddenly we were connecting in words and flirting with eye contact. We talked until long after the munch was over and the others had gone home. Just before he was about to ask me out (according to him), I excused myself and went off to the bathroom. When I wheeled myself out from behind the table, I realized from the look on his face that he hadn't seen the chair at all until that moment.

I cried in the bathroom, telling myself that while it had been a nice fantasy, now he was going to make an excuse, tell me that I was pretty, and scoot off never to be seen again. Which was exactly what happened, and the story might have ended there except that he called me later in the week. He'd been too shocked by my disability to make a decision, but the more he thought about me—so he told me when he called—the more he wanted to see me again. He got my number from a friend and made a date. I wanted him to see how I lived so that if he was going to bug out, he'd do it quickly, so I invited him to my house for dinner. He ended up staying the night, and doing some light SM play with me.

Having sex with my lower half is always an ambivalent experience. It makes me sad that I can't feel it, and the fact that I wear adult diapers is a problem. A lover has to be very careful with me, because if I'm not lubricated enough I'll tear and bleed, and may not heal right since I spend so much time sitting. However, most guys go straight for the vagina because it's there. My Sir, on the other hand, spent two hours doing mild bondage and torture on my breasts, and noticed that I orgasmed twice from it. Instead of going for my lower half, he concentrated on fucking my mouth and tits, and I came from that too. Afterward, he told me that he loved fucking my face and tits because they were so much more "me" than just some holes in the lower half. Some dominant men might like reducing a girl to faceless holes—I can understand the thrill of objectification. My Sir would rather use the parts of me that are sensate and paying attention to him. He'd rather look in my eyes while he takes me, and I love that. Eye contact is a big part of our sex, even when my mouth is full of him.

My Sir travels a lot for his work, and he is not interested in having a live-in wife. She'd probably spend a lot of time alone and lonely anyway, and she wouldn't like the fact that he prefers not to own a lot of things or establish a household. He lives with a lifestyle couple who are his good friends, and he can have the luxury of a nice house on the days when he's home without having to worry about upkeep. I've got my full-time job plus I do commercial artwork from home, so I'm pretty busy too. We both figured that we were too career-oriented to have spouses, but we suit each other fine.

When he's gone I'm doing my creative work and I'm not pining for him. I usually hear from him every couple of days over phone or email, and he often asks me to check things for him on the Internet. I'm his Miss Moneypenny when he's away, and his courtesan when he's back. When he's coming over, I put all my work and art aside and make myself completely available and submissive to him. It's wonderful, we both get the best of both worlds, and I am Rosamund to his King Henry.

My disability does make it more difficult to go places, especially his home where there are a lot of stairs and no way to get me up them. That's why he comes here—I've only actually been able to get to his room once, because he carried me. We both decided that my condo was far more comfortable—it's prettier, the bed is bigger and nicer, there are no roommates, and of course no stairs. I keep all the toys at my house, so that they can be on hand when he wants to use them on me. We can go to most restaurants together, although usually we order in or I cook something nice for him, and he feeds me bites of it. He likes me to ask sweetly for each piece of food from his fingers. My submission makes him light up, and I love to see that.

He does tell me what to wear when he's around, and I wear my hair in the style and color he likes. Other than that, I manage my own life and my own medical affairs. He isn't interested in running that part of my life, and acknowledges that I know better than he does about my medical care, and I'm more compliant with treatment than he is. (Must be that dom/sub thing!) When I was in the hospital with phlebitis problems, he flew home and was there for me, and texted me in both airports. So I know that he cares—I'm not just some woman to fuck, I'm his geisha on wheels. I don't know where our relationship is going to go, but I'm taking it for all that it's worth. We're not together because I am desperate or have low self-esteem and he's using me. We're together because we are shockingly compatible.

Tonight he is coming out again. He's home for the next three days and is going to spend much of that with me. I'm going to greet him at the door draped in a sheer red veil, with a cold glass of wine held between my breasts. I'll sparkle in the light of his love, and he'll shine in mine. My body's defects don't matter. My wheels are just the delivery system for my devotion.

Winning The Battle

Angel Lincoln

The first introduction many people have to the Master and slave lifestyle comes from reading books and short stories, and watching movies. In these types of material, the Master is eternally strong, confident, in good health, and always ready to have sex. The slaves are skinny, healthy, flexible and able in take large amounts of pain. No one is ever sick, the kids are not in the next room waking up, and the dog is not jumping on the bed. The Master is not exhausted from a long day of work. The slave is not on her period and having cramps. They can kneel for hours with no pain in their knees. No terrible life-altering experiences happen in the books and movies. The tales end with great sex, orgasms, and everyone living happily and healthily ever after.

Then a would-be slave finds someone in real life to try all the great things they saw or read. When the Master has a few days of being exhausted from work and does not play with the them, they may start to question themselves as a slave. *In all the books and movies, the Master is always ready to play with slaves, so what is wrong with me? I must be a bad slave. I have disappointed my Master.* Or they may go another route and decide this person cannot be a Master because they are not living up to what the slave had expected. Similarly, when the slave has a bad day and can't get into the mindset that the Master expects, they also start to question their ability as a Master, or their slave's suitability. When real life falls into new Master/slave relationships, it can cause failure if both of the parties believed it would be just like the movies and books.

Master/slave is really about a relationship between two people who want these roles, no matter what. The Master is in charge of the home, providing and caring for the slave; the slave takes care of the Master's wants and needs, and knows their place in the relationship. Master/slave is about power exchange; the kinky sex and fun bondage games are just how this couple might enjoy their sexual times. The real day-to-day world keeps spinning, and it often gets in the way. The best we can hope for is that we each remember the dynamics of our relationship in those times.

If the relationship is strong and the couple is together for a long time, other factors come might into the relationship—kids, old age, health issues, money problems, and lack of energy for sexual play. These are the times the relationship is tested. Obeying when it is easy and fun does not take a lot of effort. Being in charge and controlling another life as well as dealing with the responsibility of another person is easy when everything is going right. But when the world starts to spin off balance, that's when the couple finds out what their relationship is really all about.

My Master and I got together 8 years ago. I was already in a wheelchair then, and both of us knew that adjustments would have to be made. Kneeling was very hard for me. Once I got on the floor, I had to worry that if I sat on my feet for too long I would get a wound. Getting back up from the floor was even harder than getting down, so kneeling was done rarely, only on special occasions. We came up with a plan; when I wanted to kneel I would lay my head on his shoulder from my chair. He knew what I wanted to do in my heart. We also had to be careful with impact play due to my lack of feeling. In the beginning my Master laid a cloth over the numb area of my back side to help him know where to hit, but as time went by, this just became something he knew how to do.

Life went well for us for about six years; many times the world would start spinning, but he and I hung on and found ways to slow it down. Sometimes the axis would become unbalanced and we would have to become creative and finds way to fix it. Then, in 2009, our world fell apart. I was diagnosed with a bone infection in my hips and back, from pressure sores I'd had in the past. Since my Master had come along we'd gotten the last wound healed. With his guidance I had not had another sore for all those six years, but the damage had already been done to the inside of my body. For those six years, unaware to either of us, my body was being eaten up from the inside out. The infection had spread throughout my pelvic bones.

In November of 2009, the doctors told me that they couldn't help, and I was sent home to die with no hope of fixing the problem. For the next six months I was in bed most of the time, in pain, with new open sores. We had to open them up each day to let the drainage escape from the tissue and bones that were being eaten away. My Master was there for me all the way, and kept telling me that everything would be all right. Neither of us would say the words "I am dying."

Finally, in March of 2010, we decided to research more and found an operation that might help me. It involved removing both of my legs and part of my hips, and we talked about how we would adjust for this, but when I went into the hospital on March 5th, 2010, we found out just how bad this whole mess was. I would need an operation, but not the one Master and I had expected. I would need what we came to know as a hemicorporectomy. The doctors told us that my legs and entire pelvis had to be removed, including all my sexual parts inside and out. I was going to be cut off just below the belly button. We were told that only about 150 people had ever had this operation, and out of those only 30 had lived. We were also told that without the operation I would be dead in six months. We had to decide what to do.

I looked to my Master to make the choice, but he told me that this would have to be my decision to make. He would gather me all the information for the pros and cons, and he promised me that he would stand beside me with either choice I made. If I decided to not have the operation, he would take me home and help make the time I had left as good as possible. If I decided to have the operation, he promised to be there for me through all the pain and tears.

I chose to live, and I decided to have the hemicorporectomy. First, this meant that I needed to have my kidneys and bowels rerouted to come out into two bags on my stomach. This operation was done April 13th 2010, and I can remember that I did not want to even look at my stomach. My Master worked with the nurses to learn how to change the bags, but I could only lay there and look away and cry while he did it. At this point, I decided all this was not fair to my Master. I told him that I would understand if he wanted to release me. I knew he would be there as my friend even if he did this. but he let me know in no uncertain terms that this part of it was not my call, and he would not be releasing me. I was still his slave, and would be even when I had only half of my body.

My Master stayed with me at the hospital almost every night. The nurses and doctors knew about our Master/slave relationship and respected it. On May 11th I had the full operation, and after eighteen hours of surgery and a couple of days of being knocked out, I woke to my Master at my side. I had tubes in me and couldn't talk, so I would do signs to say "I love you" to him. I was in the hospital a total of eight months before I could go home.

It is now 2012, and he and I are still together. Most of the play side of the lifestyle is not something he and I can do anymore, but we keep trying to find ways I can still enjoy some type of sexual experience. I still have times when I cry, thinking how unfair all of this is to my Master, but he keeps on being wonderful. For example, I have a special bed to sleep in, to support my body. I thought he would put this bed in our spare bedroom, but he put it in his bedroom. When I asked why, he let me know that he understood my fear of abandonment and he would not have me in another room. I was his slave, and even if I could not be in his bed, I would be in his room close to him. I can still serve him food and coffee, and spend time with him doing many things— reading, playing games, talking about life and enjoying the time we have.

I believe that what helped us to stay together is that we had so much in common besides sex and play. Our relationship was based on a power exchange, and that does not change because you lose half of your body. He still leads me and owns me, and I still know my place in our relationship. I still have days when I cry and wish things could change, but I am a lucky slave to have the Master I have. I've talked to a few of the other people who have had this operation, and only two others were lucky enough to keep their spouse. Most of them lost their loved ones; the whole ordeal was too hard for them to stay together.

My Master is not only my Master, he is my hero. He has stood beside me through all of this and never complains about our Master/slave relationship not being like the books and movies. He has encouraged me to find new ways to feel successful—I am now in college and work with other amputees to help them as an advocate. I may have only half of my body, but I could not ask for a more understanding, caring, devoted Master.

It's especially hard when old age and health prevents us from doing what we feel our role in the relationship calls for, but that's when we have to be creative. We have to come up with new ways to serve, and we have to learn to communicate with words what our bodies no longer allow us to do. If you want to kneel before your Master to serve him a cup of coffee but, your body does not allow you to do the act that is so strong in your heart, you have to find a way to let him know what your heart wants to do. He knows his slave's abilities, and he will understand. For example, a slave could lower her head while she is serving him. They will both know that what she is really doing in her heart and mind is kneeling. When the Master has become ill and does not have the strength to flog the slave for an hour, she can learn to understand that the ten minutes he does flog her is the best expression of his desire that he can give. Each person can learn to understand that the other is still giving one hundred percent of what they *can* give, and one hundred per cent of what someone is capable of is worth just as much as them giving one hundred per cent back before life slapped a curve ball on them.

Master and slave relationships have to do with the mind and heart. No matter our age or disability we can still give one hundred per cent of our heart to our Master. A Master can still lead their slave, even from a wheelchair, and a slave can still kneel in their heart and in their Master's mind without ever leaving their own wheelchair.

If you can still love and obey, and if the Master can still love and lead you through the hard times, you can win the battle.

The Care And Feeding Of A Disabled Submissive

On Keeping A Disabled Slave
Mistress Fae

So you've got yourself a disabled submissive or slave. Maybe they came to you already disabled, and you thought you knew what you were taking on, but now that you've got the collar on them, you're not so sure. Maybe they're under consideration, and part of that is you taking the time to figure out if you can work around their disability and still get enough of both people's needs met. Or maybe—worst of all—your long-term sub has been in an accident or come down with a disease, and your lives have been completely upended. You may both be wondering if you will have to jettison your power exchange relationship, if it will be just another casualty of the problem. Like your sex life, your SM life (if you're into that), and your social life. You may be staring down the barrel of that gun and wondering how you're going to master anyone in the face of this pressure.

Well, I can't guarantee you that your sexual, SM, or social lives will survive, but I can guarantee you that your Master/slave or Dominant/submissive relationship can definitely survive, if you work at it. Ours did. I have two boys, and both of them are disabled. Brian is my husband and slave of sixteen years, and Lou is my "new" slave of four years. I also had a slave for a few years who had serious kidney disease and needed dialysis every other day at the end, before he died. It was in looking after this slave that I learned how to master a slave with disabilities and profound medical difficulties, including being their advocate in hospital situations (a task which I will discuss shortly).

Brian became disabled in a car wreck in 1987; he collided with a lorry and since then has been getting around mostly with forearm crutches, although we have a chair for when he is tired. (I fitted it out with subtle hard points to cuff him to when I'm taking him to a play party on a difficult day for him.) He spent so much time typing during his long recovery period that he gave himself carpal tunnel syndrome, and has had operations for that as well.

Lou came to me as a RAF veteran, injured on duty, with shattered leg and shoulder that had been rebuilt, but never were exactly right again. He gets around with a cane, and also has insulin-dependent diabetes so we have to be careful with every loose nail on the floor. When I do SM with him, I can't break skin or leave heavy bruising because it will take him so long to heal. One of the reasons that he offered himself in service to me was because he saw me with Brian, and he figured that I couldn't be too hung up on having slaves with perfect bodies if I was keeping him around.

Keeping disabled slaves is not an easy thing, but I find it to be morally rewarding. First, someday we are all going to be old and wrinkled and at least somewhat decrepit, and we shall have far less value in the relationship market when that happens. Those who believe that the aforesaid relationship market is anything but utterly unfair are simply privileged, and their privilege hasn't yet been revoked by time and circumstances. It's inevitable that we will fall off the high end of people's fantasies, unless we go out and get hit by a lorry while we're still young and healthy and beautiful, at least those of us who were ever that way. (Although I read this bit aloud to Brian and he pointed out that he'd already had that happen to him, and he was still continuing to live, so perhaps I should pick another example?) There are a small number of unblemished and healthy potential partners, all being fought over by far too many people, and then there are a much larger number of perfectly wonderful individuals in the equivalent of the scratch-and-dent bin whom no one is picking up, because they're all far too busy judging books by their covers. Their loss, my gain, and the gain of those Mistresses and Masters who aren't afraid to take on a slave who is a little worse for wear.

I find it uplifting when I can figure out a way for a slave to serve and please me that is well within their capabilities. The look on their face when they realize that they did it, and did it well, is priceless. It is wonderful to know that I not only made them feel worthwhile in their position, I extracted something excellent from a source that had been tossed aside by someone less perceptive. It's a victory on all counts. Of course, the service that they render me has to actually be something that pleases me—if it is only me humouring them, it is an insult to both of us. If I don't want what they have to offer, it is up to me to find out what they can offer that I want, and train them in excellence at those skills. To give them make-work and then put up with the result suggests that I am not a competent enough Mistress to discern and draw out their talents, and also that they are entirely useless and not worth training. This attitude does no favours for either party. It's better to ask them to do the three things they can manage than to come up with twenty more that you don't really want from them.

For me, taking on a disabled slave also means taking on their illness or injury as well. I own them, all parts of them, and I want to know how best to use them. This begins with an in-depth study of the parts of themselves they like the least, and they may fight you a bit when it comes to looking at all the pain their conditions have caused. This is especially true for my slaves, both of whom are strong, competent men who have suffered terrible and unfair setbacks. However, if I am to own a vehicle, I'd best know how fast I can't drive it, and what sort of oil it requires to keep going. I'd also better know at least something about what's under the hood, and if it has "special" qualities that require gentler handling, I'd better know about that as well.

Step by step, I've taken control of their bodies, problems and all. Because, you see, you don't really have control over someone's body until you have learned exactly how to use it, in every way. So the following list is the procedure I suggest for the owner of a disabled slave to get hold of the situation.

+ First, learn everything you can about your slave's condition. Become an expert on it. Read up on symptoms, including the unusual ones, and ask them which ones they suffer from. The Internet is useful here—for every syndrome, there's a support group with a website. Your local library is useful as well, and your librarian can order you all sorts of books. Rather than owning a tonne of books where I really only needed specific sections, I took books out of the library, copied the relevant sections, and put them in a three-ring binder with colour-coded tabs so that I could find information quickly. (Or, rather, I made *him* organize them into a binder with colour-coded tabs. That's a good task for a semi-sessile sub to do.)

+ Read up on medications, including all the side effects. Read up on possible meds they haven't taken yet (for example, meds for potential future problems or worsening of symptoms). All the information for medications and their side effects are online in one place or another. I recommend www.drugs.com, which has over 5000 listings, including side effects.

+ Start going with them to their doctor's appointments. You can say that you're there for moral support, or to help them remember everything (you might want to have a notebook and paper to take notes if you're using that excuse), or just that you love them and you want to be sure that they're getting the best possible treatment. If they've got long-term doctors who know them well, have your slave introduce you. Act supportive of them. Doctors like to see that their patients have supportive partners who care about them and their progress.

+ If they are going to a support group for their condition, go with them—other people in the support group may have ideas that you can add to your box of tricks, or their partners may have some. (For example, sexual positions for people with limited mobility—things the doctors aren't going to cover.) If they aren't going to one and don't want to, it might be worth it for you to go yourself a couple of times, if only to mine up more knowledge. Assuming that "partners-of" are welcome, people generally react very positively to the idea of a partner looking for ways to be more supportive. They don't need to know the nature of your relationship, only that you care and you want to know more. Of course, if there is an actual partners' support group, try there first, but it's often useful to hear people with the same condition talking about it. They may have a different way of looking at it.

+ If your slave is on disability, find out how that works. Add the info to your library. If something goes wrong with state aid at the worst possible moment, you may need to be their advocate, and it's best that you know everything about it in advance. If they aren't on disability, research it anyway in case something happens and they can no longer earn their own income. Despite popular ideas, most masters and mistresses are not independently wealthy and supporting hordes of indigent slaves. Even if you're supporting them, the household could use the extra income.

+ While you're at it, learn the ins and outs of their health insurance program as well. Again, if something goes terribly wrong, you may need to be their advocate. More than one partner of someone with disabilities has ended up standing in a hospital arguing with an insurance company about whether their beloved was going to get lifesaving treatment or die. Seriously, if you are the dominant in the relationship, this is very much your job. Arm yourself in advance with all the knowledge you can find.

+ Check with every government agency about benefits for people with your slave's problems. There are a number of public and private programs out there that no one ever hears about unless they know the right people. Doctors are sometimes clueless about these things—social workers, governmental department staffers, or the medical benefits staff in hospital may have a better idea. There may be useful programs that your slave isn't taking advantage of, or is too intimidated to ask about. (This is especially important if you unfortunately happen to live in a country without national health care.)

✦ This may sound strange, but if you have a full-time owned slave, it may be useful to look into coping mechanisms used by parents of children with the same disability as your slave. While your slave is (we assume) a competent adult and not a child, I did find a lot of useful information there. It is one place where you can hear people talking about how to deal with a disability in someone they are entirely responsible for, and how that feels.

✦ On the same subject, a study was done in Finland about the coping skills of parents with disabled children, and translated into English. High-coping families generally had parents who were adaptable, were sensitive to non-verbal cues, were able to reframe situations to seem more positive, and— most important—had an extensive and excellent support system. This advice is something that any master of a disabled slave should take to heart.

✦ The study also quoted the parents as saying that the best emotional support of all were other parents who had children with the same disability. When I read this, I went looking for other dominants whose slaves were the same boat as mine, and I advise you to do the same. There's nothing like talking to someone who really understands the situation, and the kind of hard decisions you'll have to make.

✦ Encourage your slave to talk to other people with the same or similar physical issues. While they may feel like the other person may judge them for their submissive lifestyle, remind them that there's a lot to talk about without getting into that subject. It's good for them to hear from others who are coping better, because they may learn new skills or coping mechanisms from them. It's also good for them to hear from peers who are coping less well, because giving support to the less fortunate reminds them how far they've come and how well they are actually doing.

✦ If your slave has an illness or injury that requires regular hospitalization, understand that you may end up being their advocate with doctors, nurses, and hospital staff. This is not because your slave is a weak individual (we hope, as they must be strong to survive these difficulties) but because someone in terrible pain or drugged with painkillers or with a tube down their throat may not be terribly effective in arguing for their own best interests. It should go without saying that if they are unconscious you will definitely have to do the work for them. Have a copy of their medical power of attorney, signed over to you, on hand. Have lists of their allergies, not just drug but food allergies as well, in large print. Tape the lists to their bed, the door of the hospital room, etc. You should make sure that such things are added to the patient's chart, but remember that medical staff often skim a chart and miss things. A large sign on the wall can be a better reminder. If you must argue with staff in order to get your slave proper care, try to simultaneously cultivate the twin forces of impeccable courtesy and implacable relentlessness. Don't get into shouting matches—you are not in power in this situation—but do go over people's heads when absolutely necessary. If you can think of a way to get your slave's needs met with the least inconvenience to the doctor or nurses, it will be more likely to be accepted.

✦ Engage in creative problem-solving. If there are mechanical problems in doing things around the house, there may be a solution. If the two of you can't think of one, open it up to your friends. They may have ideas that you don't, especially if they are logical engineering types who can observe the environment and figure out a way to make things easier. For example, neither of my slaves can stand to do the dishes, but putting a chair or stool in front of the sink puts them too far away to reach effectively. I had a carpenter friend tear out the doors under the sink and set them further back, and install a seat at the right height and distance that could swing out and then back when no longer needed. I also installed a pull-out spray faucet for easier handling.

✦ Have the right tools on hand for them to be able to do their jobs. There's a lot that someone can do with the right tools—a slave who can't type can do Internet research for you if they have a voice program. A slave who can't sweep the floor can use a vacuum cleaner if it's built in the right way. Adaptive devices can help in many ways; make the investment. You'll all be glad that you did.

✦ Of course, the final chapter is having a slave die while still in your service. I'm personally of the opinion that if a slave becomes terminally ill on your watch, you owe them whatever care can be given until the end. You don't have to do it alone, and indeed this is where a household of slaves (and perhaps other masters, or other lovers and friends) really comes into its own—both as a team to share the load and as support for you as you grieve and cope. I was incredibly grateful that I had two other slaves at that time, and that they cared about their "slave brother" enough to nurse him through his last days with loving attitude, and not just because I'd ordered them to help.

✦ Have advance directives drawn up for your slave, in case of a disease that eventually takes their lives. If they have another partner, make sure that you are both in agreement as to what should happen to them, and also that you are in agreement as to who should make the decisions about it. This issue should ideally be decided well before Death is hovering over the hospital bed. Regardless as to whether you or another partner is in charge of their fate, you should be gracious and supportive to the other partner, and let them know that you appreciate their pain and value their emotional needs in the situation. It's a sad fact that the air over a hospital deathbed is all too often the place where buried family resentments explode, so do your best to ameliorate the situation in advance.

✦ Have your advance directives drawn up in case something happens to you. I know too many Mistresses and Masters who died suddenly and left their slaves with no contingency plan, no support, and no legal right to be in their late owner's house. While some couples are legally married, even those could use a contingency plan. A disabled slave will have a harder time relocating to a new home and life, especially if they are used to living in a home that has been adapted for their needs. If you have been supporting them, they may find themselves suddenly needing to face bureaucracies and get on disability payments. It may help to have a friend who can walk them through that process, should the worst happen.

✦ The same case applies should you need to release them, or if they decide to break their contract and leave. Even if they have angered you, it is part of your honour as their Mistress or Master to leave them as independent as possible, with some kind of support system. You are a role model—don't forget it, even if they do.

✦ Find ways to talk with your slaves about their disabilities that involve humour and compassionate jesting. If we don't keep laughing, we shall certainly all begin to cry, so laughter is crucial. It might help to have affectionately amusing terms for the symptoms that plague them, and the tools that they depend on. This is especially the case for symptoms that are embarrassing or humiliating, such as having to wear an adult diaper or not being able to use one's legs to crawl around the room.

✦ At the same time, if you can help them to eroticize something endemic to their condition, do it. Many slaves have a wonderful ability to eroticize helplessness, which can contribute beautifully to your power exchange if they can feel good about that instead of worthless. Others can eroticize humiliation and embarrassment, such as the aforementioned situation with adult diapers and crawling around. If the two of you can find a way to turn something that is humiliating in a bad way into something that is humiliating in a positive and erotic way, even if it is only when you two are alone, do it. This can provide your slave with something to hang onto when times are physically rough. Remember that one of the best reasons that a slave might venture into a new fetish area is that their dominant finds it arousing. If you can sincerely lead the way there, they will follow.

✦ Slaves with disabilities often end up going through regular medical procedures which can often be frightening and uncomfortable, and humiliating in the negative sense. Giving them some token to remind them of the relationship during these times can help strengthen their resolve and comfort them through unpleasant operations and procedures. While metal collars and chains are generally a problem with X-rays and MRIs, your mutual imaginations should be able to come up with alternatives. Putting them in frilly panties (if they are male) or other sexy underwear, or no underwear at all can be one reminder; knotted leather thongs tied firmly in private places can be another. Even simply writing something on their body with marker where only they can see it (such as "You are my property") would be an alternative. One master created a special "glyph" to write on his slave's body that combined the words "brave" and "slave". Some slaves may prefer something nonsexual, or may fear that a more sexual reminder would cause an unwanted and humiliating (in the bad way) erection during examinations or procedures. Others may prefer a sexual reminder because its pleasant associations counter the unpleasantness of the situation, and remind them that in spite of everything wrong with their bodies they are still sexual beings. Some may even welcome a certain amount of mild arousal as an antidote to painful but necessary proceedings.

✦ If you have a sexual relationship with your slaves, it's important to keep it going even in the face of illness and injury. First, sex has an analgesic effect. Even if it seems like it's impossible to get into a sexual space while ill or in pain, if you actually manage to get through it to some kind of release, it can be of great benefit in terms of pain relief. That doesn't mean that the mistress or master of a disabled slave or one with chronic pain need only keep the slave well fucked and they won't need pain medication, but it can provide temporary relief in some cases.

+ Beyond the practical effects, regular sex whenever possible shows the slave that they are desirable beyond the obstacles of their physical condition. It is all too easy for someone with a disability to feel unattractive and sexually worthless; this is not helped by our society's tendency to see the disabled as nonsexual people. Keeping your sex life going helps them to resist slipping into such a mindset. After all, if this wonderful dominant clearly wants them, how bad can it be?

+ Remind your slaves—and yourself—that sex is whatever you want it to be. Society says that sex isn't really sex unless it eventually involves putting a penis into a vagina (or some equivalent if you are not heterosexual), preferably with the penis-person on top. We perverts know better. Sex doesn't have to involve penetration, or genitals, or even orgasms. What it does have to involve is emotional satisfaction of some kind. Use your imaginations and work toward finding erotic activities that are emotionally satisfying. This may involve getting over some cultural programming about what makes a "real man", a "real woman", a "real dominant/master" or a "real submissive/slave". Root those messages out of your psyche—or, better yet, if they are your slave's internal messages, find ways to arrange a scene so that they are challenged and shown to be ridiculous. Then reward them with a non-traditional but very satisfying sexual activity.

✦ Some conditions give a better pain tolerance. Some make a slave unable to bear any S/M pain at all. Bondage may also be difficult, especially for long periods of time. Pain medications may interfere with a slave's ability to process strong sensations. These situations all need to be handled with compassion and sensitivity. However, with that said, if your slave is a masochist and can bear it, there is a lot to be said for forcing the body to make its own endorphins for temporary pain relief. Chronic pain conditions can wear out a body until it seems like no endorphins can be made; I've found that this can be helped by trying entirely different forms of pain. For example, pain that mimics the deep ache of an arthritic body—such as bruising or "thud"—may not inspire a flood of endorphins, whereas something like needle play might. Also, keep in mind that if the genitals are turned on, the body is able to endure more strong sensations.

✦ If your slave's disability involves chronic pain or chronic illness, or other problems that wear them out, you may have to walk a fine line between pushing them out of a slump and giving them the chance to rest when they are overtired to the point of irritability. That's one of the hardest choices about being a master or mistress in general, and especially so for a disabled slave. Sometimes, all they need is a good push to get them out of a self-pitying or fatalistic rut. Sometimes that push will send them over the edge into hysterics or collapse, and what they really need is some tender care. Sometimes being made to do their daily service in spite of their pain will boost their self-esteem. Sometimes they just don't have it to give you, and being faced with failure at a given chore will make them feel even worse. You, as their owner, will have to figure out which approach is best each time. Make it a day-to-day decision: accept that what worked today may not work tomorrow. If you make a mistake, learn from it and move on.

Usually the best preventative for such mistakes in the future is to get your slave to communicate better with you and with their body, so as to give you all necessary information.

A disabled slave is not necessarily so much more work than an able-bodied one, if they have the right personality and true service mentality. I have had much more trouble and much less faithful work out of many so-called slaves who were perfectly able-bodied than I have gotten out of my boys. I am reminded of the valet in the first season of the series "Downton Abbey" by Julian Fellowes, where the master at first thinks to fire his lame war-veteran valet, but then thinks better of it, as he is the most honorable servant who has held the job. I myself have always been the sort to enjoy finding treasures among the dross at flea markets, and that's really the same mentality that it takes to own one of these special slaves—an ability to see potential, and to draw it out. Once it's done, you are far more proud of your own skills as a slave-handler, and far more proud of them, and that pride is communicated between both of you in everything that you do together.

In Memory
Master Kal D.

This is a short essay, because Joseph was only in my life for a short while. I wish that I was able to write volumes about what a great slave he was, and how he worked hard to overcome his challenges in order to be a slave worth having, but the words fail me. Joseph was part of our leather family for four years. When he came to me, he was nearly entirely deaf from a rare form of neurofibromatosis, which is a pretty rare disease as it is. Fibromas had formed on his aural nerves, and slowly robbed him of hearing. They also caused dizziness and headaches, and occasional aphasia. That means that he'd forget how to use words sometimes, and would speak with gestures, when he couldn't even remember ASL.

That didn't stop him from being a great slave, though. Joey could express surrender with his body in a way that made it completely clear. He talked with his body more than most slaves communicate with their mouths, and unlike mouth-talking, his communication was always painfully honest. He was pretty homely, too, lean and whip-thin with a wide craggy face and a prematurely balding head. The baldness was especially hard for him because he had some skull malformations from childhood surgery, so he usually wore a hat of some sort. But while I like a pretty boy as well as any other gay man, I know better than to judge on the basis of looks, especially when it comes to a slave to clean your house and look after your things, as opposed to a nice body to have fun with and perhaps never see again. My other two slaves, Geo and Hal, aren't beauty queens any more than I am, but we all have a great time and a lot of hot sex anyway. Faithfulness doesn't always come in a pretty wrapper.

How do you help a deaf slave to serve you? Joey had a vibrating beeper that I had him always wear on his belt. When it went off, he knew that I wanted something, and he'd report. If he was turned away from me I could set it off from across the room with my own beeper. While his brain was still sharp, he was great at doing my accounts and other computer scut-work, and he could fix practically anything.

We developed our own special protocols. Joey had learned some ASL when he'd begun to lose his hearing in his teens, so we developed a series of hand gestures that were derived from ASL, but not exactly the same, because we didn't want the occasional deaf person to accidentally see how I was ordering him around in public. When I wanted something, at first I would make eye contact with him, but of course accidental eye contact happens, and that was confusing for him. So I made a rule: If I made eye contact and smiled, it was just a "hello, slave, I like looking at you," but if I made eye contact with no smile, it meant that I was about to give him an order. On the few occasions when I was unhappy with him and had to discipline him, I didn't give him any eye contact. I just looked beyond him, or only at the parts I was punishing. We communicated through eye contact more that we ever did through hand signals, so that was really hard for him, perhaps worse than a beating.

During play, he would often go pretty nonverbal, or have trouble remembering how to form useful words. I gave him a golf ball to hold in his hand, and to drop as a safe word. I usually gagged him when I wasn't using his mouth, because he liked to have something to bite down on, and also because I think he was aware of the weird noises he'd make—his last dominant had apparently commented on them—and he was self-conscious about it. I didn't mind, but he did. He didn't speak often because he worried that his voice was high and flat and loud. Well, maybe it was, but we didn't care. However, by the end we were carrying on most of our conversations in ASL, or even just random hand gestures.

If there was one thing that bothered me about Joey, it came out of my own insecurities. I feared, on some days, that I was a second choice as a master. I knew that Joey was bisexual, and that he'd turned to men at an early age because it was easier to get sex from men, but I always worried that he'd really prefer to serve a woman. It was the one subject he wouldn't communicate on. He was just as loyal as could be, and I had no complaints, but when I "lent" him out to help dominant female friends, he lit up like a Christmas tree. I could see how much he loved it, and also that he feared he'd never get more than passing attention from a woman because he was a homely little deaf guy who fell over periodically. I figured that their loss was my gain—I got a great slave who was loyal to the core.

Over time, the dizzy spells got worse and worse, as did the aphasia. Some days he couldn't work, but on his good days he was still very proud of being able to serve me. I remember the last day that he served me by himself—my other two were out of town, and it was just Joey and me. He was having trouble deciphering my notes—the aphasia was spreading to reading words by that time—and understanding me, which was a new thing, but we kept on going. He was so proud to be able to make me dinner anyway, and to keep the house spotless. And we could still communicate in the language of flesh, of touch and surrender. His disabilities didn't affect his cocksucking one bit, nor his ability to take a caning.

My other two slaves did have to pick up the slack for him during that time, but they didn't mind—Joey was so friendly and affectionate that they loved him too. In fact, when the brain tumor—caused by the neurofibromatosis—was discovered, they insisted that we keep him home and take care of him through treatment. When the treatment was ineffective—the tumor was found too late—they insisted that we care for him in his last days. He was also HIV+, and while he'd staved that off for a long time through healthy living, the brain tumor knocked everything down and the virus ran rampant. Joey lasted four months after the doctors told him that there was no point in more chemotherapy, and died at home with the three of us. That's what a family is for—standing by each other until the end.

Perfect Beauty, Perfect Grace
S. Leonard

I've got two slavegirls living in my home and serving me. Allison, my alpha slave, is able-bodied and has been living with me for almost twenty years now. She works as a legal secretary at small local firm. Laurell, my beta slave, has cerebral palsy and has been in an electric wheelchair all of her life. She has some mobility in her limbs and can feed herself and grip some things, but her hands have tremors. She has a bit of a speech impediment, which makes some people think that she is less intelligent than she actually is, but that's their insulting assumptions. Laurell has been with us for five years now and is an excellent slave, by my standards.

When I say "serving", I need to clarify that. We aren't much for "service" as most people see it. The house gets cleaned by a professional that I pay, twice a week. We also have a friend who comes in as a hired nurse for Laurell about every other day—she is also a slave, but not mine; she belongs to a friend and we were happy to hire her, because she understood our situation. I don't keep slaves because I want free housecleaning. I keep them because I love to see a woman surrender fully to me. My girls are both pleasure slaves. My rule for them is Strive For Perfect Beauty and Perfect Grace.

So what does that mean for a crippled woman, to be blunt and non-politically-correct? How can she have perfect beauty with her diminished body? How can she have perfect grace with her spastic limbs? It's possible. When I say "perfect beauty and perfect grace", I don't mean the physical body. I'm talking about the attitude. I mean that when I come home every day, my girls are smiling and happy to see me, and completely focused on me. I mean that when I want something, they are happy to give it to me. I mean that when I touch them, their bodies react to my touch with complete surrender. I mean that they work toward having a good attitude even when it's hard. This state of grace is not easily achieved—it takes a lot of continual work and self-discipline and dedication—

but it is just as achievable by someone who can't walk as by someone who can.

Laurell first came to us as a roommate, because we happen to have a house with a wheelchair ramp from the former owner, and it's all very handicap-accessible, and we had this one spare room right off the ramp. Allison and I knew that she identified as submissive, and we offered to take her under our protection and vet all her potential partners. She accepted, although she did comment that she didn't have any potential partners, nor was likely to. I told Allison to do what she could to buck Laurell up—to make her feel some confidence in her ability to attract people in spite of her CP. I commented to Allison that Laurell was certainly cute, and had spunk and charisma. Allison later told me that it flashed through her mind, "Then why don't we keep her for ourselves?" but she didn't say anything at the time.

The two of them became friends, and I discovered later that they were plotting together to get me to take Laurell on as a slavegirl myself. Allison kept mentioning it, and Laurell kept being there and being charming, and it didn't take me long to figure out that I'd be a fool to pass it up. In my defense, I waited long enough to make sure we could work out the details—Laurell needs a lot of help in her day-to-day activities, and since Allison and I both work full-time jobs, other people have to come by and help her out. She is our "house slave", and there are still plenty of small jobs she can do for us. She answers the phone and takes messages while we're gone, she makes coffee for us in the morning and evening, and she periodically sends me little messages throughout the day that lift my spirits. Allison and I both come home for lunch, and Laurell has it ready—we buy pre-made lunch items that she can easily assemble or microwave. It saves money, time, and allows me to spend my lunch break with my girls instead of waiting in line alone at some cafeteria. I do have her transcribe my notes and interviews for me, but much of her day is spent doing volunteer writing for a disability organization.

When people find out that Laurell is my slave, they get some pretty odd looks on their faces, even if they are also into the scene. I can tell that some of them are wondering whether I'm keeping her against her will—as if her disability prevents her from leaving. As if I just let her move in and then informed her that she couldn't leave, and she bought it. Others wonder if she became my slave out of low-self-esteem, because she thought she couldn't do any better, or couldn't make it in the outside world. Some wonder if I am fetishizing her disability—if the fact that she is crippled makes me hard. There's an assumption that I couldn't possibly be interested in having sex with her unless I had a specific fetish for her condition. Which is insulting to both of us.

Laurell is small—we estimate that if she were able to stand she'd be just under five feet—and lightweight enough that I can lift her easily out of her chair. When we play or have sex, I can pick her up like a compact little bundle of woman, and do whatever I want with her, and she can't physically resist me. (Not that she ever wants to, I should point out. Her surrender is genuine; she tells me so with her whole body.) Do I find that helplessness sexy? Hell yes. Do I believe that her disability makes her intrinsically helpless? Hell no. I know how hard Laurell has worked to survive and find her way through life. She grew up striving to be a "supercrip", to be as independent as possible. She dealt with conflicting messages all her life—do what the doctors say and don't argue versus stand up for yourself and talk back, even when they are dismissive of you because of your disability. It took a huge act of courage for her to come to terms with her own submissive nature, to understand that it didn't stem from her disability—she'd be this way even if she'd been able-bodied, and has met people with her condition who are dominant—and choose to surrender to me. I don't see that surrender as a mere side effect of her condition, because *I know what it costs her.*

Playing with Laurell at public play parties is a double-edged sword, especially where there are a lot of strangers who don't know us. Some people are profoundly uncomfortable at watching me torment this tiny crippled woman. They feel that I ought to be treating her like a delicate toy, to be kept in a box. They really don't like it when I tip her out of her chair onto the floor and flog her while she's wriggling around on the carpet. (We usually put her in a push-chair instead of her electric chair when we go to play parties, and handcuff her to it, to emphasize that she is a slave here and she will go where we push her.) But the people who instinctively want to protect her don't understand that she doesn't want their protection. She wants *my* protection, to protect her from their well-meaning intentions, and to play with her in a way we both enjoy.

We usually let the DMs meet her and talk with her beforehand, and they run interference if people complain. On the one hand, I'm always hyper-aware of people's glances when we play publicly, and of people's discomfort. On the other hand, I kind of think it's good for them to see someone with a different body getting to play the same way as anyone else in the place. We joke about how we are a public service. When we really feel like provoking people, I'll taunt her while she's on the floor, telling her that she can't get away from me. She trusts me enough that it's not triggering for her, and we both agree that sometimes triggering the watchers a little gets them thinking.

I know that sometimes life is pretty hard for Laurell, in spite of everything we do to make it easier. But life can be hard for anyone, and it's no excuse for turning away from her personal discipline of Perfect Grace. I get angry sometimes when life is unfair to me, and I don't take it out on my girls who are so vulnerable to me—that's my discipline, the other side of Perfect Grace: Perfect Honor. To say that she shouldn't have to strive for her goal because her body doesn't work all that well is also an insult to her. To tell someone, "We'll make allowances for you, don't bother to try hard," is to say, "You're weak and useless." I would never set Laurell up for failure with a physical task, but it's her central nervous system that's damaged, not her mind or her willpower. I expect her to rise to the challenge, and she does. That's not seeing my slave as weak, it's seeing her as strong, and asking her to live up to the strength I see in her.

And that's what I'd tell a dominant who's going to take on a disabled slave: Find the areas where they are capable, or could be capable, and expect excellence in those areas.

Be realistic about it, but remember that believing in someone can push them further than you can imagine. Once you've established yourself as their dominant and their authority—once you can say, "This is so," and they accept it—you can tell your slave that they will be excellent in this area, and they will do it. They may be surprised at themselves, but if you're mastering them properly, you'll be surprised at how hard they'll try.

To a disabled submissive who wants to be a slave, I would say the same thing: Find a dominant who is willing to push you. It may be the case that you've been throwing yourself so hard against your disability, against the things you *can't* do, that you've probably overlooked a whole lot of things you *can* do. It may be that facing down the *can'ts* has made you feel like there are a lot more of those *can'ts* than reality would suggest. Find a master who can figure out what you *can* do, and who will push you to achieve excellence.

Back From The Edge Of Death
Karl Ardane

If this title sounds dramatic, it's because I almost lost my slave ... before I really had him.

I met Lee years ago in a leather bar, and we had an on-again, off-again relationship for about a decade. It went "off" periodically because of Lee's behavior. We were egalitarian partners who played with SM—I'm a top and he's a bottom, and we had ferocious sexual chemistry. The sex was always magical, and we hoped it would carry us through the hard times ... but Lee would go off and party, and I'd stay home worrying about him. He'd go through periods when he'd drink too much, do too many drugs, and have a lot of promiscuous sex. The latter led to him picking up a few annoying but curable venereal diseases, and I kept rescinding my body fluid privileges because I was worried he'd get drunk and pick up something not so curable. He also smoked, and he'd quit while he was with me, and then take it up again when he left.

Lee had endured a hard childhood. His parents were abusive alcoholics who threw him out when they found out that he was gay. He was like a deer that constantly bolted; that street kid in him was still strong even in his forties. We'd be doing fine—or so I thought—and suddenly he would flip out and start the cycle of drinking, drugging, and partying all over again. After a period of this, sometimes we'd break up, or I'd wake up and find him gone off to another city. Maybe he'd leave a note. Maybe he wouldn't.

Then there was a period where I didn't see him for a few years. I shacked up with another guy who claimed to be a slave, but when push came to shove he didn't follow through. He was happy to get beaten and fucked, but balked at being told to do my laundry or run errands. By this time, I knew what I wanted, and it was more than just another cute butt to play with. I wanted a real slave. I wanted someone who would actually surrender completely to me and do what they were told, and I set out interviewing submissive men with that in mind.

It seemed like the universe was playing some kind of joke on me when Lee came back into my life. After all, wasn't he the exact opposite of what I was looking for? Except that the sexual chemistry was as strong as ever, and after our first yeah-OK-we-might-as-well scene, he confessed to me that part of the reason he kept running away from me was because he was afraid. Some part of him wanted to submit completely, and that terrified him, so he would run. He pointed out that his running usually came right after some really intimate SM, when I'd been able to get inside his head. But that urge had gotten stronger over time, and he'd ended up trying out full-time slavery with another man while we were separated. Problem was, he'd picked a jerk. After it ended badly, he decided to try again for my doorstep. "I figured that if I was going to have any hope of doing this right, I'd better be doing it with the best man I knew," he told me. And I was sold.

Of course, it wasn't nearly as smooth sailing as I hoped. We drew up our contract, set out all our expectations, and made the rules. It was delicious … for a little while. I loved being in control of him; it filled a deep abyss inside me that I hadn't even known was there. But then I'd press him in some way that reminded him of his parents, and he'd resist, and rebel, and then bolt. Twice he ended up running away from me. The first time, he came back the next day. The second time he ended up at a friend's house for days, and the friend misunderstood our relationship and feared that I'd become abusive. It took weeks to settle that straight, and by this time I was so angry at Lee that I gave up. I figured that we'd given it a good try, but he just didn't have it in him to obey me. His fears were stronger than his desire to submit, or will to commit.

He came back after about a month—I remember that it was January—and begged me to try once more. He made promise after promise, but I was having none of it. We sat there in the corner booth of a little restaurant and tried to make sense out of what had happened, while the snow fell outside. Finally, against my better judgment, I agreed. "But if you run again," I said, "we're over. Never come back. I can't go through this one more time." We decided to wait two weeks, and then we'd spend a weekend in Fort Lauderdale and I'd collar him for one last time. He'd thrown away the collar I'd bought him last time, anyway, so I'd have two weeks to replace it.

But that weekend never did happen, because I was awakened by a phone call later that night. Lee had had a heart attack, and he was in the hospital. The frightened guy on whose couch he was crashing called me, clearly relieved that I was willing to come down and take care of things. I remember spinning around the room, terrified—and then something resolved inside me. I made one stop between my apartment and the hospital, and it was at one of those giant hardware supply stores that was open all night. I bought a chain and a lock, and went to Lee's bedside.

Standing in the hallway, the doctor told me all about his health problems. Lee had ruined himself fairly thoroughly with alcohol and drugs and smoking and other unwise choices. He was forty-nine and needed a bypass, which would be performed as soon as he was stable. He was beginning to develop COPD from his smoking, which he'd scaled up while living away from me—his former "master" had given him cigarettes as rewards for good behavior. The doctors feared that he might be developing a pulmonary embolism. He'd had bone loss from drugs and was developing osteoarthritis in his shoulders and legs. His entire lifestyle would have to change if he was to survive, they told me. He wouldn't be able to do the activities that he was used to—in fact, he'd be something of an invalid, and would find it difficult to get around.

I went into the hospital room where Lee was just coming around. We told each other that we loved each other. Then I held out the chain, his new collar, and said: "I've changed my mind. I'm going to collar you right now, unless you tell me not to, and I'm going to take you as my slave and run your life. I'm going to make sure that you do whatever it takes to stay alive. Understand that leaving me is not just a choice to stop being my slave—it's a choice to die. I know you, and I know that if you're left to run your own life, you will kill yourself. You won't last six months. So there it is: be my slave, or I leave you to your death. What will it be?"

He looked at the chain, and said, "Yes, sir." I locked it around his neck and sat with him. He told me that he believed this was the universe giving him a heads-up, a final choice. To turn it down would be crazy.

Lee's been my slave ever since. I did have to take the chain off his neck later that night, because he couldn't have it in surgery, but it went back on his neck as soon as he got back home after his bypass. Actually, that chain is a good example of how living with a disabled slave requires us to find good compromises. Because of his breathing difficulties, he can't have anything heavy around his neck any more. So I cut it in half and made it into bracelets, and he has a light webbing collar instead.

Our sex life isn't as crazy as it used to be—SM is harder with COPD and a bad heart, but we still manage to do some activities. Anyway, what attracted me to Lee wasn't that he was a masochistic pig, but that his response was so intense—and it still is. Some of his medications make it difficult for him to regularly achieve erections, but in response his body has learned how to come from getting fucked. With his cock in an on-again, off-again state, he finds that he is less sexually selfish and more interested in getting me off.

There were other compromises as well. We had to give up the rent-controlled apartment that I loved and move into a more expensive one, but it's at ground level and he doesn't have to cope with stairs. It has wide doorways in case we need to get a wheelchair through it, and we put a chair in the bathtub for him. Since he's home on disability instead of working, he spends time puttering around each day and doing what chores he can. The wheelchair (which we have in case of emergencies) is often put into use by him wheeling baskets of laundry around, or moving other things that he doesn't have the strength to lift.

He does what he can—I'm not shallow, and I know what it cost him to surrender to me. I'm not going to complain that he can't lift a trashbag. If all he could ever do was get me coffee and suck my cock, I would be all right with it. I make all his medical decisions and control his diet and exercise, and you can bet that he's been clean of everything not doctor-prescribed since his collaring. He would sometimes forget his medication, so I carry his med-minder with me, along with an alarm, and he eats his pills out of my hand like a dog eats treats. That makes it easier for him to cope with those copious amounts of pills—he admits that he looks forward to it now.

Lee has had to adapt to a whole new life in the seven years we've been together as Master and slave, and he admits that if I hadn't collared him that night and taken over his life, he would be dead now. Instead, he is a well-loved slave. I know that I am probably going to lose him well before I go, but it has been worth it. I've tamed this wild deer, and while it may look to others like he is now caged, it's not by me. He is caged by the results of the choices he made. With me, he finds ways to be free in spite of it. Really, we set each other free.

Show You

Rafael Z.

For Delia

I want to show you
just how much you can do.

I want to take you somewhere
you've never been.
I don't want to keep you in a box
like you've been keeping yourself
all these years
I was never any good with the toys
that need delicate keeping
and though you pretend to be
the precious china doll
I can smell that underneath
you're really that stuffed creature
whose soft fur and bright eyes
I always came back to
after the other toys were broken or outgrown.

I want to haul you out of your box
and rough you up some
drag you through the mud a little
convince you that you're sturdier
than you ever dreamed you could be.

I want to take you to the circus
on a field trip, to my friends' houses
I want to sleep with my head pillowed
on your devotion
I want you to keep the bad dreams
out of my life
and I know you can do it

I want to make you believe
it's OK to be a little worn
around the edges,
a loose joint or two,

a missing eye or ear,
or even a limb,
some stuffing leaking
and lumpy in places.

I want you to think of that
not as being imperfect
but as showing the world
how much you are loved
because I want to own you
and I want to squeeze
the stuffing out of you.

I want you to remember the rabbit
and the skin horse and that lesson.

I want to make you Real.

I want you to take my hand
even though it scares you
even though it might hurt
I want that trust, it is my liquor,
the burning trail down my throat.

Take my hand and I promise
I will show you
just how much we can do.

About the Editor

Raven Kaldera is a queer FTM transgendered intersexual shaman who is often seen with a cane and occasionally with leg braces or in a wheelchair. He is the author of too many books to list here, including *Dark Moon Rising: Pagan BDSM And The Ordeal Path* and *Power Circuits: Polyamory In A Power Dynamic*. He and his beautiful and useful slaveboy Joshua have been teaching and presenting workshops regularly for many years to the BDSM, Neo-Pagan, Sex/Spirituality, transgender, and a few other communities. He sees his physical challenges as just another obstacle to overcome in his quest to change the world whenever possible. His slaveboy Joshua refers to himself as "a wholly owned subsidiary of the vast enterprise that is Raven Kaldera." 'Tis an ill wind that blows no minds.